ON SELF-HARM, ATONEMENT, A VULNERABLE CHRIST

Reading Augustine

Series Editor:
Miles Hollingworth

Reading Augustine offers personal and close readings of St. Augustine of Hippo from leading philosophers and religious scholars. Its aim is to make clear Augustine's importance to contemporary thought and to present Augustine not only or primarily as a pre-eminent Christian thinker but as a philosophical, spiritual, literary, and intellectual icon of the West.

Volumes in the series:

ON SELF-HARM, NARCISSISM, ATONEMENT, AND THE VULNERABLE CHRIST

By David Vincent Meconi

BLOOMSBURY ACADEMIC
NEW YORK • LONDON • OXFORD • NEW DELHI • SYDNEY

BLOOMSBURY ACADEMIC
Bloomsbury Publishing Plc
1385 Broadway, New York, NY 10018, USA
50 Bedford Square, London, WC1B 3DP, UK

BLOOMSBURY, T&T CLARK and the T&T Clark logo are trademarks of
Bloomsbury Publishing Plc

First published in Great Britain 2020

Copyright © David Vincent Meconi, 2020

David Vincent Meconi has asserted his right under the Copyright, Designs and
Patents Act, 1988, to be identified as Author of this work.

For legal purposes the Acknowledgments on p. x constitute an extension
of this copyright page.

Cover design by Catherine Wood
Cover image © Simon Li / Getty Images

Bloomsbury Publishing Plc does not have any control over, or responsibility for,
any third-party websites referred to or in this book. All internet addresses given
in this book were correct at the time of going to press. The author and publisher
regret any inconvenience caused if addresses have changed or sites have ceased
to exist, but can accept no responsibility for any such changes.

A catalogue record for this book is available from the British Library.

A catalog record for this book is available from the Library of Congress.

ISBN: HB: 978-1-5013-2620-2
         PB: 978-1-5013-2621-9
       ePDF: 978-1-5013-2623-3
       ePUB: 978-1-5013-2622-6

Typeset by Integra Software Services Pvt. Ltd.
Printed and bound in the United States of America

To find out more about our authors and books visit www.bloomsbury.com
and sign up for our newsletters.

CONTENTS

desiderantibus evanescere ...

FOREWORD

It is hard to overestimate the importance of Augustine's work, both in his own period as well as in the subsequent history of Western philosophy. Until the thirteenth century, when he may have had a competitor in Thomas Aquinas, Augustine was the most important philosopher of the medieval period; and the impact of his thought continued through the Reformation to our own day. Many of his views, including his theory of the state, his account of time and eternity, his understanding of the will, his attempted resolution of the problem of evil, his exposition of God's knowledge, his theory of language, his approach to the relation of faith and reason, and his investigations into the human psyche have remained influential up till the present time.

One thing that is distinctive about Augustine's thought and that makes it sound disconcertingly contemporary is his insightfulness into the complexity of the human psyche. The fragmentation of the self is a recurrent theme in his work, and he is perceptive about the distance introduced into human relations with others because of the internally divided human psyche. What is even more impressive about his keen observations is his account of the self-alienation resulting from such internal divisions in the self. Augustine's idea that a self-alienated person will loathe himself and in fact will seek determinedly his own destruction is striking.

Although all of Augustine's work has been the subject of extensive scholarly study and reflection, there has been less investigation of Augustine's powerful observations about self-loathing. And yet in our own time we certainly are in a position to appreciate his wisdom in this regard. How is it possible that a human being would find comfort in cutting herself? How is it possible that a person would return repeatedly to an abuser? Or to self-undermining addictive behavior? The answers to these and similar questions require not just a psychoanalytic theory of human self-destructiveness; they need explication from within a whole worldview that undergirds a distinctive account of human nature and the true self of a human person. And that is what David Vincent Meconi, S.J., has undertaken to do in this new book on Augustine's philosophical and theological account of the human psyche. Meconi is a well-known Patristics scholar whose previous work has focused on the thought of Augustine. His many articles and books on Augustine have tended to concentrate on Augustine's account of the human person, and that extensive expertise is in evidence in this new book on Augustine and self-harm.

Meconi begins by describing in detail Augustine's view of the world and of human beings in the world. Foundational to all Augustine's understanding of human nature is the belief that the world has a Creator and that human beings are made in his image. What is noteworthy about Augustine's view is the additional claim that human beings are made for union with their Creator. A human person is not only made by God but is also meant to be united to God in the giving and receiving of love.

On Augustine's view, as Meconi painstakingly shows, without this relation to a loving God a human person tends to fall apart, to want and not want the same things in internal fragmentation. For Augustine, a human person in this condition is in effect trying unsuccessfully to be self-sufficient, to be for himself what God should be for him. He is thus in effect trying to be God for himself. But the effect of this effort is the opposite of what a human person is intended to be. As Augustine sees it, a human person is by nature suited for deification in union with his Creator. In turning his back on his Creator to become sufficient for himself, a human person becomes not more than human but less. Like Narcissus in the old myth, a human person who rejects the love of God becomes destructive to himself.

Meconi focuses on the much-discussed episode in Augustine's Confessions of the theft of pears to highlight both the oddity and the insight of Augustine's view of that theft. As Augustine tries to show through his probing questions about that theft, the person in love with himself apart from God is in effect loathing himself through his self-love. True self-love is manifest in the giving and receiving of love in union with God. Apart from that union, self-love and self-loathing are yoked so that a person seeks the self-destruction he hates. Meconi's ability to describe and defend Augustine's position elucidates Augustine's view of the human predicament so that it resonates with contemporary concerns. When the great wealth of the industrialized and secularized Western nations leaves those nations also with high rates of suicide and depression, Meconi's presentation of Augustine's analysis of the human condition is apt for our times.

In the book's last chapter, Meconi brings into the discussion Augustine's view of the central doctrines of Christianity, the Incarnation and atonement of Christ. In his sensitive explanations of a complicated part of Augustine's thought, Meconi makes evident that, for Augustine, human beings cannot by themselves conquer their tendency to spiral into self-destruction. The richness of this part of Meconi's work defies any easy summary. He sketches Augustine's views of the distinction between self-loathing and self-denial, the historical importance of Christ's crucifixion and its on-going impact on the Church, the role of surrender in self-fulfillment, and the communal nature of human well-being. The importance of Augustine's views on these topics to current thought is evident, and Meconi's expert exposition of Augustine's views illuminates them and sets them in the broader context of Augustine's whole worldview.

The result of Meconi's labors is thus an excellent book. With his far-ranging familiarity with the works of Augustine, from the letters and sermons to the major treatises, Meconi makes Augustine's thought alive and intelligible so that it becomes available for wrestling with now. This book will make a difference to all those who care about Augustine or the topics that moved him and that animate us still.

Dr. Eleonore Stump
Robert J. Henle Chair in Philosophy
Saint Louis University

ABBREVIATIONS AND ACKNOWLEDGMENTS

LIST OF CITED AUGUSTINE'S WORKS[1]

Abbreviations	Latin Titles	English Titles	English Translations	Latin Editions	Date
c. Acad.	Contra Academicos	Against the Skeptics		CCL 29	Nov. 386–Mar. 387
b. uita	De beata uita	On the Happy Life		CCL 29	Nov. 386–Mar. 387
ciu. Dei	De ciuitate Dei	City of God	William Babcock (New City Press, 2013)	CCL 47–48	413–27
conf.	Confessiones	Confessions	Maria Boulding (Hyde Park: New City Press,1997)	CCL 27	397–401
diu. Qu.	De diuersis quaestionibus octoginta tribus	On Eighty-Three Varied Questions	Boniface Ramsey (New City Press, 2008) America, 1977)	CCL 44A	388/96
doc. Chr.	De doctrina Christiana	Teaching Christianity	Edmund Hill (New City Press,1996)	CCL 32	396; 426/27

[1]Taken from the standardizing list offered at *Augustine Through the Ages*, xxxv–xliii.

en. Ps.	Enarrationes in Psalmos	Expositions of the Psalms	Maria Boulding (New City Press) 6 vols: Ps 1–32 (III/15) 2000; Ps 33–50 (III/16) 2000; Ps 51–72 (III/17) 2001; Ps 73–98 (III/18) 2002; Ps 99–120 (III/19)2003; Ps 121–50 (III/20) 2004	CCL 38–40	392 (1–32) through 406/07 (119–33), sporadically up through 422
ench.	Enchiridion ad Laurentium de fide spe et caritate	The Enchiridion on Faith, Hope, and Charity	Bruce Harbert, Enchiridion as in Christian Belief (New City Press, 2005) 264–343	CCL 46	421/22
ep.	Epistulae	Letters	Roland Teske, Letters (New City Press) 4 vols: 1–99 (II/1) 2001; 100–55 (II/2) 2003; 156–210 (II/3) 2004; 211–70 and Divjak 1–29 (II/4) 2005	CSEL 34, 44, 57, 58, 88	cf. Fitz- gerald, s.v., Epistulae, Augustine Through the Ages, 299–305
ep. Jo.	In epistulam Joannis ad Parthos tractatus	Tractates on the First Letter of John	John Rettig, Tractates on the First Epistle of John (Catholic University of America Press,1995); second half of vol. 5	SC 75	406/07
ep. Rm. inch.	Epistulae ad Romanos inchoata expositio	Unfinished Commentary on the Letter to the Romans	Paula Fredriksen Landes, Augustine on Romans: Propositions from the Epistles to the Romans and Unfinished Commentary on the Epistle to the Romans (Chico, CA: Scholars Press, 1982)	CSEL 84	394/95

Abbreviations	Latin Titles	English Titles	English Translations	Latin Editions	Date
f. et symb.	De fide et symbolo	On Faith and the Creed		CSEL 41	Oct. 8, 393
Gn. litt.	De Genesi ad litteram	On the Literal Interpretation of Genesis	Edmund Hill, On Genesis (New City Press, 2002)	CSEL 28.1	401/15
G. litt. imp.	De Genesi ad litteram imperfectus liber	On the Literal Interpretation of Genesis, an Unfinished Book	Hill, On Genesis	CSEL 28.1	393/94; 426/27
Gn. adu. Man.	De Genesi aduersus Manicheos	On Genesis, Against the Manichees	Hill, On Genesis	CSEL 91	388/89
gr. et lib. arb.	De gratia et libero arbitrio	On Grace and Free Will		PL 44	426/27
gr. et. pecc. or.	De gratia Christi et de peccato originale	On the grace of Christ and Original Sin	Roland Teske, Answer to the Pelagians 1(I/23) (Hyde Park: New City Press, 1997)	CSEL 42	418
Jo. eu. tr.	In Johannis euangelium tractatus	Tractates on the Gospel of John	John Rettig, Tractates on the Gospel of John (Catholic University of America Press) 5 vols: 1 (1–10) 1988; 2 (11–27) 1988; 3 (28–54) 1993; 4 (55–111) 1994; 5 (112–24) 1995	CCL 36	406/21?
c. Jul.	Contra Julianum	Against Julian	Roland Teske, Answer to the Pelagians 2 (I/24) (Hyde Park: New City Press, 1998)	PL 44	421/22

c. Jul. imp.	Contra Julianum opus imperfectum	Against Julian, an Unfinished Book	Roland Teske, Answer to the Pelagians 3 (I/25) (Hyde Park: New City Press, 1999)	CSEL 85.1 (bks. I-III)	429/30
lib. arb.	De libero arbitrio	On Free Will		CCL 29	387/88–395
mor.	De moribus ecclesiae catholicae et de moribus Manichaeorum	On the Catholic and Manichean Ways of Life		CSEL 90	387/88
nat. et gr.	De natura et gratia	On Nature and Grace	Roland Teske, Answer to the Pelagians 1(I/23)	CSEL 60	415 spring
ord.	De ordine	On Order		CCL 29	Nov. 386–Mar. 387
pat.	De patientia	On Patience		CSEL 41	417/18
s.	Sermones	Sermons	Edmund Hill, Sermons (Hyde Park: New City Press) 11 vols:1 (1–19); 2 (20–50) 1990; 3 (51–94) 1991; 4 (94A–147A); 5 (148–83) 1992; 6 (184–229Z); 7 (230–72B) 1993; 8 (273–305A); 9 (306–40A) 1994; 10 (341–400); 11 (Dolbeau's Newly-Discovered) 1997	CCL 41	cf. Aug. Through the Ages, 774–89
Simpl.	Ad Simplicianum	To Simplicianus		CCL 44	396

Abbreviations	Latin Titles	English Titles	English Translations	Latin Editions	Date
sol.	Soliloquia	The Soliloquies	Kim Paffenroth, Soliloquies (Hyde Park: New City Press, 2000)	CSEL 89	Nov. 386–Mar. 387
spir. et litt.	De spiritu et littera	On the Spirit and the Letter	Roland Teske, Answer to the Pelagians 1 (I/23)	CSEL 60	412
Trin.	De Trinitate	The Trinity	Edmund Hill, The Trinity (New City Press, 1991)	CCL 50/50A	399–422/26
uera rel.	De uera religione	On True Religion	Edmund Hill, True Religion as in Christian Belief (Hyde Park: New City Press, 2005) 15–104	CCL 32	390/91
c. Faust.	Contra Faustum Manicheum	Against Faustus, a Manichee		CSEL 25	398/400
c. Iul.	Contra Iulianum	Against Julian		CSEL 25	421
c. ep. Man.	Contra Epistulum Manichaei quam uocant Fundamenti	Against the "Foundation Letter" of the Manichees	)	CSEL 25	396/97
cat. rud.	De catechizandis rudibus	On the Instruction of Beginners	***check on this	CCL 46	399/405
diu. qu.	De diuersis quaestionibus	On Eighty-Three Varied Questions	Boniface Ramsey	CCL 44A	388/90
quant.	De animae quantitate	On the Greatness of the Soul		CSEL 89	388

The author would like to thank Fr. Allan Fitzgerald, O.S.A., James Wetzel, Jonathan Yates, Anna Misticoni, and all the wonderful members of the Augustinian Institute at Villanova University, where these reflections on the infamous pear tree first took root. Many of these pages stem from "Ravishing Ruin: Self-Loathing in Saint Augustine," *Augustinian Studies*, Volume 45, Issue 2, 2014, pp. 227–46. By kind permission of T&T Clark, much of Chapter 5 originally appeared in the author's "Augustine's Thinking on the Atonement: Identity, Appropriation and Transformation," *T & T Clark Companion to the Atonement*, ed. Adam Johnson (London: T&T Clark, 2017) 381–8. The author would also like to thank his immediate ecclesia for their illuminating insights as these thoughts were being shared and expressed: Dr. Sue Harvath, Fr. Dan Shaughnessy, Dominican Sisters of Mary, Mother of the Eucharist, Julie Ann Desmond Olsen, Fr. Richard Buhler, S.J., and Fr. Christopher Collins, S.J. The author is especially thankful to his friend and colleague at Saint Louis University, Eleonore Stump, for her gift of counsel and her gracious Foreword presented herein.

INTRODUCTION

As I was walking to my departing gate in the St. Louis airport not long ago, the main ideas for this book were just coming to mind. What happened in the next few minutes put these pages into print. As I was making my way, a very large and powerful-looking man with a most offensive t-shirt walked directly toward me. Sporting a shirt depicting a nun spewing vulgarities with her middle finger obscenely outstretched ("F**k you, F**k the world"—without the asterisks—she was portrayed screaming!), he approached. Looking out from behind my Roman collar, I wondered how I might diffuse what looked like a rather ill-disposed encounter, to say the least. As he drew nearer, I tried to appear poised and asked, "What's up with the shirt?" Weighing in around 250 pounds of solid muscle, and about 6 and ½ feet tall, his swagger suddenly came to a sheepish stop. Like a little boy, he immediately looked down to the ground, and softly confessed, "Father, I hate myself so much, I want everyone else to hate me too."

His eloquence and self-knowledge amazed me. He went on to relay all the horrific decisions he had made since he had fallen into a life of violence, drug abuse, and sexual sins of all sorts, quickly concluding that God must really hate the kind of person he had become. "On the contrary," I assured him, "the fact that you would walk up to a Roman Catholic priest in the middle of a busy terminal and confess all the things wrong with your life, tells me that there is still grace in your soul. God is far from giving up on you!" We talked, and I then asked him if I could give him a blessing. We both had tears in our eyes, we prayed together for a few seconds and, reaching up, I made the sign of Christ's redeeming and ever-merciful cross firmly on his forehead.

About ten minutes later as I waited for my plane, an older gentleman came over and told me point-blank: "I'm going to call the police and have that man you were talking to arrested. That is the most offensive t-shirt I have ever seen." After he calmed down a bit, I responded:

You're right, it's a terrible shirt. But that's precisely what he wants: he wants you to hate him so he has a reason to hate even more and so lash out at you. However, if you were to talk to him, you would find out that he really is searching for some forgiveness and the last thing he needs is one more person telling him he is no good.

Dissatisfied, this man left me to my crossword, but reappeared just a few minutes later. "Father," he gleefully reported, "he turned his shirt inside out." Now bumped to a flight the next day, I walked out of the airport and noticed my contrite penitent sitting with a reversed tee shirt gazing out the window onto a Midwest sunset. At that moment, I had a deep realization that Augustine was right once again. This time I understood how the Bishop of Hippo knew that wherever we feel unloved and unwanted, we continue to loathe and lacerate ourselves through a seemingly unbreakable cycle of sin and destruction. Yet, we begin to be brought back to health once we allow compassion and truth into our divided hearts in order to be loved and finally healed.

Looking back at the rawer moments of his life, Saint Augustine of Hippo (354–430) expressed how he too was in love with his own ruin. Like this hurting penitent in front of me at the airport, Augustine knew he sinned where he was unwilling to risk the vulnerability of relationship, preferring instead to collapse into himself. Such disintegration is one of the sure signs of hatred, finding ways to make oneself or the other disappear. Hatred seeks to obliterate any signs of those we have come to hate. All traces of that person are henceforth to be removed and we work hard to banish that one from our lives and memories. In those obviously painful years of seething adolescence, Augustine came to hate himself and, consequently, to find an acid joy in destroying himself, in ravishing his own ruin. Only by destroying any good apparent in himself, could he feel better about his own malice. By ruining all the beauty in him, he could more easily cozy up to his own cruelty. But in loving his own sorrow in this way, Augustine admits that he not only "sought out whatever could cause me sadness," voyeuristically drawn to watching tragedies he himself "had no desire to undergo." In this doleful turn inward, he inevitably came to be resentful of the one true Shepherd who alone could lead him out of the barrenness of self-loathing into the pastures of freedom: "I was an unhappy beast astray from your flock and resentful of your shepherding, so what wonder was it that I became infected with foul mange?"[1] Loving the unlovable inevitably

---

[1] *conf.* 3.2.4; Boulding, *Confessions* (I/1) 77.

renders such a one so fragmented that he or she is simply unable to receive another, especially Love himself.

This is concupiscence for Augustine and in his understanding of salvation; Satan and his angels rebelled against love out of sheer self-centeredness and their reluctance to allow God to be the heart of their world. In this rebellion, Augustine detects not only disobedience but the deeper wounds causing such an act of pride, envy, and self-loathing. When one feels like "used goods," what is one more outburst, one more sinful act, one more overindulgence, one more splurge? Since I'm already broken, what does it really matter anyway? These are the sorts of questions I hear behind every confession: I am a sinner and I know I in no way deserve the Father's forgiveness. It is this sense of disappointment in oneself and despair before love that the enemy of our human nature longs to exploit.

Not content to remain among angels only, the devil enters God's good creation in order to entice human persons to turn away from God as well. He does this furtively and cleverly, not lying to the first humans but exploiting their desire for God by promising they can become "like God" without any help from God (Gen 3:5). This is why Augustine understands all sin as attempts at self-deification. When we freely turn away from God, we inevitably set ourselves up as his rival equals. For example, in community life, when I need the stationary we hold in common, I simply take what I need, even if it is the last piece. But if I go into the common room and there is no stationery left, I secretly curse my brother who would have taken the last sheet, the last envelope. When I am selfish, I figure, "Well, I'm busy and need this right now." When I am inconvenienced because the stationery shelf is empty, I think, "Certainly we could be more mindful of one another," inevitably relishing anger against another for doing the very thing for which I just excused myself. In this way Augustine sees the fall as the means by which created persons willingly seek their own perfection without inviting in the Perfect. In so doing, we cannot help but inflict alienation upon ourselves. How so? Sin removes every soul from community, rendering the fallen one content to live in a world obviously broken and bankrupt, but at least it is his or her own ruin.

Here the fallen grow comfortable with being at the center of their own world—devoid of intimacy, true enough, but at least now they can do whatever they want, whenever they want, and however they want. While this alienation and subsequent autonomy may lure and fascinate for a while, it cannot stand. It has to be replenished. This is the vicious cycle of sin: it collapses further and further into itself. It is here the true nature of evil is realized: a dissolution that leads to isolation and the consequent disgust of oneself. In turn such disgust leads to a self-imposed alienation and a fracturing not only of one's own internal well-being, but even the relations that have brought that person meaning and delight.

This is how Augustine understands sin, and this is what the following study seeks to understand more deeply. Sin sabotages the relationships of community, yet we continue to embrace the very thing we know brings us nothing but sorrow after the fact. We consequently nuzzle up to that late-night bowl of ice cream; we indulge in that extra drink we don't really need; we find ourselves returning to the latest gossip, or to the clicking of numbing internet images. This allure to decay is the unfortunate irony of sin, but what is even sadder is that we freely choose it. At some depth deep down in our fallen soul is a morose love of our own ruin, a hatred of our own wholeness. I may know that the world I am creating at this moment is not great, but at least it is *mine*. And so, I end up wanting what I really do not want.

Augustine of Thagaste came to this realization early on, recorded by the meta-moment of his stealing some otherwise insignificant fruit. Looking to inject any kind of excitement into an otherwise lackluster late summer day, the young Augustine finds himself and other like-minded wastrels eager for some excitement. Chancing upon a neighboring farmer's orchard, the youths ransacked some low-hanging pears—not out of hunger or even out of storing them for later, but simply to destroy not only the fruit, but their inner selves as well. Augustine lived in a world that looked very different than ours today, but his soul still speaks to any contemporary. He was gifted with an uncanny insight into the depths of the human condition, realizing profoundly what an enigma we can be to ourselves. So, while most of us today no longer spend summer days in orchards and roaming in open fields, we can still well relate to Augustine's awareness of how he was magnetized to his own melancholy, in love with his own dissolution, and strangely found comfort in the uncomfortable.

Once we know how to name this sort of confusion, it is a sad mockery easily detectable each day. It is the teenager who cuts her flesh simply in order to be reminded of how life still pulses under the numbed surface. It is in the children who have grown so accustomed to an adult's demeaning words; they begin to internalize their own unworthiness and slowly begin to look unhealthily elsewhere for affirmation. It is the older gentleman who does not feel at all worthy of care, so he refuses to ask for help with his basic human needs, sitting all alone never wanting to be a "bother" to a loved one. We have all grown friendly with that which destroys us. We have all secretly believed that just this once, that binge or puff, that drug or carnal pleasure may finally relieve our cravings. We know it won't. But we do it anyway. Why? Aware of our ugliness, our inadequacies, and infidelities, none of us feels truly worthy of perfection and the joy promised in Christ. Consequently, how often we very secretly and subtly convince ourselves that maybe, just maybe, this time that cigarette, that momentary condescension, that harsh word might, this time, finally satisfy me. Maybe this idol, which I can keep under my control, can this time be an adequate substitution for the God I cannot control. In such fallacious reasoning we cave, and that repeated vice only deepens our shame. Once weakened, we figure since we have already fallen, what are a few more supposedly harmless peccadilloes, and so it continues. This is the puzzle these pages seek to decipher. Why would one fall in love with one's own decay and freely embrace meaningless pain and suffering? Why do we repeatedly find a sin attractive even though we know deep down that it will only disappoint?

Most of this book was written in the latter part of 2018, and during that fall semester I was also teaching a first-year theology course here at Saint Louis University. One of the assignments I give my students every autumn is to imitate Augustine's *Confessions* as they lift and prayerfully examine one scene from their own life's story. I am always struck by what pain so many of these young people have endured; but I am even more struck by how resilient they are in the face of the modern world that functions on reducing them to consumers or supermodels, and usually both. This past semester, one of my students began her paper with a paragraph that captured so much rawness that I asked her if I could share it here. As I reflected on her words, I could not help but hear a twenty-first-century Augustine who only hated himself more and more as he looked down to see those pears doing nothing other than rotting away for no reason. My student wrote:

> Initially, there is a primal part of you that screams in protest—but even the life instinct of the body can fail in the end. This kind of temptation is especially horrific to those who do not understand, but to those who experience it daily, hourly, by the minute and *second*—it is even more so. I cannot begin to describe to *anyone* what entices me to drag a blade down the skin of my arm for the mere sensation it brings, nor the emotions that arise within me at the sight of my blood. There are no words to explain what it is like to have this seductive yet simultaneously terrifying entity in my head that *roars* for me to gorge myself on every single damn morsel of food in sight,

then belittles me for doing so immediately after and whispers for me to put an abrupt end to my existence, when my stomach bursts and my throat burns and my face is soaked with tears. I cannot force any individual to grasp what it is like to live every single day dreading the next: treading carefully around someone who is supposed to love and nurture you, analyzing and scrutinizing every word you speak, every motion you make while interacting with family, friends, peers, professors, employers, and strangers for fear you will fail and offend and be hurt, working yourself to the bone because these results are not perfect, not ideal, because you are not good enough, *never good enough*, struggling to breathe because you are faced with societal norms that you do not conform to regardless of how much you *yearn* to—too fat, too overweight, too obese, anxious, unworthy, disgusting, pathetic, repulsive, *broken*—to be loved, valued, adored.

Without serious intervention, such a cycle of self-loathing remains endless. For Augustine, the needed healing begins with proper confession, like a modern-day therapist who would no doubt advise those like my student here that, "Maybe you need words instead of blades or knives."[2] Confession takes us into a deeper understanding of who we are—wounded and errant, yes, but when we allow the words to flow forth and allow ourselves to be known, we see ourselves even more truly, beloved, and made for eternal communion. My student's words in this assignment aided her in this process of healing and transformation. She came to see Augustine's point that where we are hurt and feeling abject, we lash out—against ourselves or others.

To examine this phenomenon of ravishing our own ruin, we proceed in five main chapters. Chapter 1 begins where Augustine always did, with God and the Christian faith's assertion that this God is a consummate community of love. As Augustine asserts so unwaveringly, the Good is always relational, whereas destruction and decay are always sadly solipsistic and woefully individual. The only thing one can call wholly one's own is one's shortcomings and destruction; everything else in the Augustinian cosmos is a matter of community and collaboration—"nothing truly belongs to me but my sins."[3] Therefore, in the first chapter, we begin where Augustine would, with the very heart of relationship. This, of course, means beginning with God

---

[2]Steven Levenkron, *Cutting: Understanding and Overcoming Self-Mutilation* (New York: W.W. Norton and Company, 2006) 80.
[3]*en. Ps.* 70, *exp.* 1.20; Boulding, *Expositions* (III/17) 435.

not as an autonomous monad, as his former Manichean and Neoplatonic theologies would have led him to believe, but as a triune community of perfect other-centered charity. After many years of inquiry, Augustine came to see how God was neither an impersonal force, however good, nor was he a Greek abstraction, however perfect. God was a community of mutual gift, the very essence of Lover, Beloved, and Love.

In the Christian narrative, sin never has the first word and it certainly does not have the last. All things are created good by Love. Chapter 2 thus looks at Augustine's theology of charity and how we created persons are all hardwired to love. Made in the divine image and likeness of triune love, human persons excel only when they find their truest selves in the other. But in the rebellion of sin, creatures collapse in on themselves in an attempt to sequester reality far from others. Here Augustine's philosophy of sin is examined more in-depth. We shall come to see how sin is attributable only to those created persons who are capable of freely turning toward the good or away from it. We may call subhuman creatures "good" or "bad," but what we really mean is that they are convenient or inconvenient to our functioning and various levels of comfort. Moral goodness or badness can be said only of other persons who have this drama built into their created souls, namely angels and humans; for only we are free to turn toward the other or turn in on ourselves. This possibility, Augustine knew, is what either stills the restless heart or allows it to wallow in its own attempt at self-satisfaction; it is what builds the City of Man or the City of God.

The first species of person to fall is the angelic. Augustine's insights into the devil's fall are carried through how he understands sin in general, for here is the paradigmatic insurgence. Adam thus comes face to face with this primal rebellion in the Garden of Eden, almost instantly involved in this civil war between God and angels. The enemy seduces Adam and Eve to sin by promising them the one state for which they were created, but the one state of perfection they did not yet have. Accordingly, for Augustine, all sin is a faint grasp at one's own apotheosis, one's own autonomous divinization. How is it we can seek to become God without God? What understanding of the divine does this assume? Augustine stands at the forefront of interpreting Satan's promise of becoming "like gods" (Gen 3:5) to Adam and Eve in a very forceful way. The narcissism Augustine detects in this seizing at divinity is not, ironically, the puffed up arrogance of the smug swaggerer, but the depletion of the anxious unable to enter into any vulnerably mutual relationship.

With an understanding of God as relational love and with Augustine's understanding of self-love in place, Chapter 3 is ready to turn to the notorious scene of his stealing the pears in Book 2 of his *Confessions*. This ostensibly harmless act proves to be a symbolic snapshot of Augustine's overall understanding of what this fallen existence of ours has become. What is intriguing for our purposes is to see how an act which (on most people's accounts of moral rendering) was fairly benign, nonetheless stands out as the epitome of human depravity many years later for Augustine. From this one scene, from this one moment when the teenaged Augustine came to realize how the restless heart could very easily be smitten with its own destruction, he came to realize deeply the sad irony of sin. Henceforth he would define sin as an attempt at self-deification which could result only in one's own destruction of self.

Relationship is risky. When a human person allows him or herself to be welcomed and embraced by another, that one no longer remains at the center of their perceived reality. For when I am truly claimed by another, I then begin to matter to another, and this carries with it the consequences of relationality and responsibility. In one way sin is easier because in that self-imposed alienation I can do what I want, when I want, as I want. I need not relinquish to grace, I remain in charge. But in this self-centeredness, the innate desire for divinization will never be authentic. Only the God-made man can make men and women gods. When the self becomes the source of one's fulfillment, however, this attempt at self-deification will inevitably lead only to division and consequent destruction. Destruction of what exactly? In Augustine's analysis of psychic fragmentation, the false gods that we set up in our lives have to be destroyed. In seeking wholeness wrongly, we inevitably establish and then abolish our own fabricated idols. What is perhaps most intriguing about this view of destruction is not that Augustine confessed hating another, but hating himself. This is the puzzle he here expresses; this is the enigma he has become.

It is a moment each of us in some way has known: the human person's inscrutable love with his or her own destruction. When quiet and honest with ourselves, each can relate to how, if not daily, repeatedly, we allow ourselves to be deluded into thinking *this or that* familiar action will finally bring us joy, and when it fails we continue to look at it longingly, just waiting for the next time we can cozy up to whatever is available in the refrigerator, when we can go shopping, or even embrace that uncomfortable tryst. We know that such things cannot bring, for they have not brought, us lasting relief from our loneliness and frustrations, but they continue to attract all the same. Pick your favorite sin; it does not matter, as this phenomenon can be detected in any destructive act. So, say, even though we know that overeating is going to lead to disappointment, drinking too much brings only a headache, gossip results in suspicion and chariness regarding who is in turn talking about us, or that masturbation (what was once tellingly named the sin of "self-abuse") will bring only frustration, the habit seems not just unbreakable, but even alluring, if even for a fleeting moment. This is what Augustine recalls when stretching back to that dark night in the vineyard. Those pears represent much more than an act of theft; they are instead signs of our fallen creature's desire to bask in our own brokenness.

"Self-love, my liege, is not so vile a sin, as self-neglecting."[4] This is the paradox taken up in Chapter 4—this relationship between self-love and self-neglect. Augustine is committed to the position that a person cannot not love. Divine, angelic, and human persons are what they are because they love, either rightly or wrongly. In the postlapsarian world in which we now live, to love rightly also means to hate rightly. This is Augustine's radical break from the Roman natural law schools in which he was trained early on: the love of self is a foundational and essential good for creatures, necessary for the continuation of life and basic survival in a hostile world. But such self-love can also lead creatures astray and have them turn in on themselves to the detriment of the community for which they have been created. This erroneous self-love is really what Augustine will call self-hatred.

Therefore, underneath any talk of deadly sin or voluntary evil is a deeper and more decisive break, the hatred of a self which cannot imagine being brought into belovedness. While ancient Christian literature in fact commends a certain *odium sui* as a way of true love, Augustine will broaden this sense of hate by defining it as loving oneself wrongly. Here we draw from the classical image of Narcissus, a handsome young man in the flower of his youth, pursued unwantingly by the mountain nymph Echo. Refusing her advances, he chooses his own reflective isolation over her reverberating cries. While Augustine does not rely on this myth directly, his understanding of self-love and self-hatred follows its main movements directly. When we refuse community, we inevitably end up overwhelmed with only ourselves. As we see in the devolution from man to flower, Narcissus represents the destruction and dehumanization that results from choosing self over the other-centeredness innate in all images and likenesses of God. That is, when one turns away from the divine in whose image and likeness one is made, the self inevitably and painfully implodes.

---

[4]Dauphin in Shakespeare's *Henry V*, act 2, scene. 4:73–4.

Instead of seeking delight in the other, the primal temptation is to collapse into oneself, knowing all along that this may not lead to the best of worlds, but at least the world I know is totally *mine*. Adam and his fallen children freely turn away from communion in order to enjoy themselves and their own plans and pursuits. This is Adam's own perversion, not the conversion God wills for his people. Sin turns one away from the God who yearns to be the center of one's life, into him or herself: "And how did this turning away come about? The human person, whose good God alone is, desired to be his own good and substitute his own self for God."[5] By choosing self over communion, the created person may find some instant delight and even a simulacrum of gratification, but the lack of true intimacy eats and corrupts his or her soul. It is in this context that Augustine preaches against this type of proud implosion. Collapsing into the self is acceptable, however, because at least now the fallen soul thinks itself free of all allegiance, all commitment, all demands. Proper self-love is not some fascination with the ego, and is certainly not reducible to the "self-care" bandied about so flimsily these days. True self-love is the basis of all other loves, the receptivity of God's loving us first (1 Jn 4:19) for we are instructed to love one another *as* we love ourselves (Mk 12:31).

In fact, Augustine is the first in the great tradition to see that there is no commandment to love oneself because we cannot help but love ourselves (Eph 5:29: "For no one hates his own flesh but rather nourishes and cherishes it, even as Christ does the Church ..."). Yet, he also consistently condemns a love of self that can establish only the moribund City of Man: "Love of self, even to the point of contempt for God, made the earthly city, and love of God, even to the point of contempt for self, made the heavenly city."[6] Given this dichotomy, we shall have to examine how the God who is love can also order his creatures to contempt, asking us to hate mother and father (cf., Lk 14:26) if we are going to follow him. There must be a kind of hatred and denial that is compatible with charity, and Augustine is expert in showing how we must love God's and not what is simply an extension of our own autonomy. We must thus "hate" family if we "love" them only as "my spouse" or "my child," and not as God's beloved son or daughter. Augustine accordingly warns us that, "it is more inhuman to love a man not for being a man but for being your son. For this means not loving in him what belongs to God but what belongs to you. Small wonder, then, if you don't get to the

---

[5]*lib. arb.* 3.24.72; my translation.
[6]*ciu. Dei* 14.28; trans., William Babcock, *The City of God* (I/7) 136.

kingdom of heaven, seeing that you love what is personal and private to you, and not what is common to all."[7]

For Augustine, true self-love can come only in Christ. Accordingly, Chapter 5 turns to the one antidote available to the sinful soul, the descent of God's Son into human flesh. Here a salvific self-love finally becomes possible, a possibility which puzzled Augustine throughout his earlier years. Later as a pastor and bishop, though, he is able to point to a type of *amor sui* as a beautiful and paradoxically relational reality: only by loving God and neighbor is one able to love oneself rightly. Now all of humanity is enabled to see the true power of the Incarnation. In becoming our neighbor, God himself orients all of our loves to himself, thereby providing the love we crave for ourselves as well. Chapter 5 traces this circularity of Augustinian charity: we can love God only by loving God's people. We love God by loving how and whom God himself loves: "If anyone says, 'I love God,' but hates his brother or sister, this one is a liar; for whoever does not love a brother or sister whom he has seen cannot love God whom he has not seen" (1 Jn 4:20). This is why the Incarnation defeats self-loathing. For in Christ, creatures begin to see not only their own worthiness precisely in their brokenness, but they also see that they too have been made Christ, another son or daughter of the Father. Augustine will employ strong language to describe this identification between Christ and Christian but in the Son's descent we are all offered a supernatural ascent into the same Father's love.

In order to know our own true love and thus our own desired wholeness, therefore, we must not only love God but love all those whom God loves, precisely because Christ has become all of us. Augustine is therefore quite adamant that loves never compete against loves, but that we come to see how true love is God's very nature. There is no merely human affection or some sort of maternal instinct for Augustine. All love is divine, all love is eternal. In other words, loving is an uncompromising and unyielding reality: persons are glued together either by their own neediness or twisted desire to control another, or they are brought together with the love who is God. For Augustine, we either technically love nothing at all or we love rightly forever. What may appear "romantic" or "maternal" or "instinctual" must, in the end, be consecrated in Christ or will prove never to have been love all along. All real love is God and such love brings the true lover to God: "Let us love each other, and we love Christ."[8] Here, in the inseparable love of God and

---

[7]*uer. rel.* 46.88; *On Christian Belief*, 88; see also, *Jo. eu. tr.* 41.8.
[8]*s.* 229N.; Hill, *Sermons* (III/6) 320.

of neighbor, the self-loathing can finally begin to know their worth, to trust their heart and their experience. In Augustine's presentation of Christ, there is no slavish obedience or empty adherence to external rules, there is only a desire for the conformity of persons. In Christ alone, then, those who have always longed to disappear can finally know their truest self.

But allowing another into our lives also means no longer being the sole arbiter and admirer of our lives. Augustine knew the power and the convoluted comfort the perverted soul can find in turning downward and seeking contentment in creatures only. Such temptation toward this settling with an idol will surely lead to corruption, and it is what the former Cardinal Jorge Bergoglio, now Pope Francis, argues stems from "a weariness with the transcendent."[9] Instead of allowing ourselves to trust the Creator in whom alone the *cor inquietum* can be stilled, we choose rather to turn in upon ourselves where it is supposedly safer and more familiar. Creatures can be controlled and we can make demands on these idols we create. But idols will never be satisfied; they clamor until we are extinguished. We may allow ourselves to enter into an alliance with another that is external and verifiable (is this how Augustine found the future mother of Adeodatus?), but internally there is no vulnerability, no real union, just the empty passing of time (and perhaps bodies) together.

Students of Postmodern theory know this phenomenon all too well. In his study on the French cultural critic George Bataille (1897–1962), for instance, the eclectic Nicholas Land calls this tendency toward a destructive solipsism the "abortion of transcendence," with the result that it is now incumbent upon each of us to create our own meaning and sense of purpose.[10] In refusing to rest in the Incarnate Son, the youthful Augustine thus creates his own hell, becomes his own hell—a lover of his own destruction, and one content to be locked in on his own pain. In my unwillingness to cry out, I may realize that I have not created the *best* world, but at least it is *my* world. "Better to reign in Hell, than serve in Heav'n."[11]

But into this corruption Perfection descends. For too long, however, Augustine could not yet imagine a love greater than his own sinfulness. He has not yet understood the power of the Incarnation and the possibility of

---

[9]Jorge Mario Bergoglio, *The Way of Humility: Corruption and Sin, On Self-Accusation* (San Francisco: Ignatius Press [2005] 2013) 23.

[10]Nick Land, *Thirst for Annihilation: George Bataille and Virulent Nihilism* (London: Routledge, 1992) 143.

[11]John Milton, *Paradise Lost*, Book 1, line 263 (Oxford: Oxford University Press, 2008) 11.

true transformation from sinfulness into sanctity. He therefore continues to live only in and for himself, refusing to allow another in. Whatever the cause of his own inability to conceive of a perfectly loving God—perhaps the harshness of his own father or the influence of Manichean dualism so early on—Augustine's sense of divinity in his years of seeking tell us more about him than it does the one true God. Christ thus appears as the only antidote to idolatry, the one in whom all true loves can be recognized and reconciled. Throughout Chapter 5, then, we come to see how the Son's Incarnation is what allows us to know, truly and visibly, God's love for us. In the crucified and raised Savior, God shows us his own brokenness so as to enter into ours.

As a result, this book is dedicated to those who want to vanish (*desiderantibus evanescere ...*), to those who are so disgusted with who they are, they wish they could simply disappear. The German Thomist philosopher Josef Pieper (1904–97) is correct in seeing how the phrase "I love you" is another way of saying, "It is good that you are; it's wonderful that you exist."[12] Accordingly, saying "I hate you" must translate into "Go away. Disappear," a wish that the other would simply vanish forever. "Let us lie in wait for the righteous one, because he is annoying to us" (Wis 2:12) is just another way of crying, "Away with him, away with him, crucify him" (Jn 19:15). Love solidifies and unites; hatred diminishes and distances. In this desire to become invisible and inconspicuous, we detect all sorts of hurtful behavior and patterns of self-harm. People who suffer from such extreme forms of self-loathing seek to leave not a trace, they make no demands, but they instead impose a distance and alienation upon themselves which removes all others from any real communion. These people are each of us, for within some part of our fallen souls, there is a voice that says we are not worthy of the Father's love, not worthy of care and compassion, and that our infidelities are somehow greater than God's mercy.

---

[12]Josef Pieper, *Faith, Hope, Love* (San Francisco: Ignatius Press [1962] 1986) 188.

CHAPTER 1
GOD AND THOSE MADE TO BECOME LIKE GOD

> Observe his inclination in yourself.
>
> — *Hamlet's* Polonius[1]

Augustine's world teemed with divinity, and cults competed: the ancient gods and goddesses of the Mediterranean, Israel's Yahweh, as well as the Triune God of the Christians all vied for recognition. The people of Augustine's time lived in a cosmos permeated with powerful numina, ever aware of the spirits which ruled the earth and skies. In one sense, Augustine himself was never *not* a Catholic Christian, recognizing that he had indeed been "regularly signed with the cross and his salt."[2] Regardless, such childhood Christianity left him with an understanding of God colorless and confused. In his best-known composition, he admits that he was first intellectually moved not so much by a desire to know the source of good, but to determine the source of evil: *From where does evil come* (*unde malum*?) was the question that moved him to seek truth, and seek he did, even if he confesses later that he went about it wrongly: "So I was seeking the origin of evil, but seeking it in an evil way …"[3] This odyssey led Augustine through various understandings of ultimate being (and for a time, even ultimate beings, in the plural), of what it means to be real, and what one's moral and religious response might be to such a commitment.

Always at the top of his class, the young Augustine excelled at most of his studies and stood apart from the rest when it came to Latin rhetoric and oratory. Youthful success translated into literary hubris, and Augustine himself admits that he found the scriptures of his mother Monica unsatisfactory, lacking in the eloquence and ornamentation he came to

---

[1]Polonius to Reynaldo, *Hamlet*, act 2, scene 1.1024.
[2]*conf.* 1.11.17, Boulding, *Confessions* (I/1) 50.
[3]*conf.* 7.5.7; Boulding, *Confessions* (I/1) 167.

expect from such figures as Virgil. Puffed up with this pride, he found the elitism of a sort of new-aged sect irresistibly appealing. These madmen (*delirantes*) who followed the Persian mystic Mani (d. 272) provided him with a quick answer to the problem of evil.[4] The Manichean cosmogony posited two deities: one good and the other evil. Such a dualism of course results in a very facile solution to evil: it is an inevitable force intertwined into the existence of all that we are and all that surrounds us. But not all is lost. To an elite few, the knowledge of stepping out of this fallen, factious order has been given. The Manicheans provided Augustine with not only a solution to his theodicy, but also with a certain level of newfound community. Here the lonely, young searcher found acceptance, along with much social advantage. Belonging to this cult instantly elevated a young upstart like Augustine into the elite imperial echelons of Roman society, as many of the Manichean elect were well connected and certainly well heeled. For nine years he allowed himself to associate with this group, but the tone of his words cannot help but suggest that he never wholeheartedly bought the Manichean story.

Yet what he would one day come to see as the providential mercy of God, the very lusts and desire for worldly gain which drove him to the heart of the Roman Empire, also proved to be the very things that occasioned a newly found respect for the intelligence of the Christian faith: "You took no heed, for you were snatching me away, using my lusts to put an end to them …"[5] Here eternal foresight and divine compassion retrospectively coalesce. For through the machinations of the high-ranking pagan Symmachus, Augustine is called to the imperial court.[6] Although, as he will retrospectively learn, he traveled northward not ultimately to serve the western ruler Emperor Valentinian II (375–92), but to meet one like himself—a man who also once found his identity in worldly strength and eloquence, yet whose life would likewise be unexpectedly transformed by wandering too closely to Christ and to his saints. For Milan was not only home to imperial intrigue, but the empire's highest political leaders were forced to share this stage with their antagonist Ambrose, the great bishop who ruled there for a quarter century until his death in 397.

---

[4]*conf.* 3.8.10.

[5]*conf.* 5.8.1; Boulding, *Confessions* (I/1) 116.

[6]The great orator Quintus Aurelius Symmachus (340–402) was a highly influential aristocrat and consul in 391, who strove to preserve the pagan practices of ancient Rome. His literary exchanges with Bishop Ambrose regarding the Altar of Victory's removal from the Roman Senate's curia are superbly symbolic of the fourth-century struggles between the Church and the Empire.

Recalling their initial encounters, Augustine marveled at three attributes: Ambrose's celibacy, his humility in reading silently, and his habitual openness to meet with the lowliest of society.[7] Of all the moments and mannerisms he could have chronicled in the *Confessions*, these three characteristics of Ambrose seemingly stood out because each of them pointed to an inner strength that only the Catholic way of living could have inspired. A celibate Roman soldier? A trained rhetorician who did not delight in the sartorial sounds of his own oratorical flare? A learned elite who opened his door to anyone who sought assistance? Augustine could not easily fathom such inconsistencies, contradictory characteristics he had never been able to fathom before he came upon the Roman Governor turned Christian Bishop.

Alongside his recognition of these personal virtues of Ambrose, also appears Augustine's appreciation for the bishop's modeling of how to read the Christian scriptures properly. He describes how he had been able to slip into the Catholic basilica and hear the great Ambrose preach eruditely and eloquently on the Christian story, particularly on those thornier passages from the Old Testament where God is depicted seemingly crudely and materially.[8] As formative as this living lesson in reading scripture properly was, this intellectual milieu of late fourth-century Milan also introduced Augustine to the story of another imperial notable, Marius Victorinus (*c.* 290–364), and his translations of the *libri platonicorum*. Whereas Ambrose provided the hermeneutic and faith community with which to read scripture properly, these "books of the Platonists" modeled for the skeptical Augustine how ancient philosophy might just aid an intelligent assent of the Christian faith. In particular, he came to learn (probably through Plotinus's *Enneads*) two life-changing truths: (1) evil was not an active substance but a parasite of the good, and (2) that there is such a thing as immaterial reality. Henceforth in Augustine's mind, God would no longer be the author of evil, nor could God any longer be imagined as an extended body, however ethereal or lissome. These new truths led Augustine to a renewed reflection on the integrity and divine destiny of the human person, and this is where we begin our foray into his understanding of sin as self-sabotage. Why so?

For Augustine, the correct understanding of the Trinity is the foundation for apprehending all of reality rightly. As we shall see, all flourishing is realized by a gift of self, an other-centeredness; whereas, all destruction is solipsistic, a self-imposed alienation away from any promise of embrace and wholeness.

---

[7] cf., *conf.* 6.3.3.
[8] cf., *conf.* 5.14.24.

Just as the divine substance is realized as *simplex multiplicitas* or a *multiplex simplicitas*, all excellence for Augustine is a matter of relationship, of being in communion with another.[9] He thus comes to see too how his own self is created to become gift. To explore these themes more deeply, this chapter proceeds in three main sections: (1) a brief genealogy of Trinitarian thought before Augustine's contribution to Christian theology, (2) after a rehearsal of this history, we shall focus on Augustine's own theology of the Trinity, and then (3) take up the human soul as a divine image and similitude of God's own inner life. Understanding how each person of the Trinity is defined by Augustine as a subsistent relationship is an essential move when we turn to his insights into human excellence and its contrary, human deprivation. As his reading of Genesis made quite clear, since every human person is made in the Triune God's own image and likeness, each created person is made to appropriate that same understanding of oneself as an other-centered person, someone now made to find his or her truest self in the gift of another.

Many great thinkers preceded him in delving into the mystery of the Triune God, and the two major ecumenical councils canonizing Trinitarian terms and concepts had already passed by the time Augustine was himself even baptized. In 325 the Council of Nicaea insisted on the consubstantiality of the Son with the Father, while in 381 the First Council of Constantinople ensured that the Holy Spirit too was as equally divine and therefore as equally worthy of worship and adoration as the other two divine persons. Yet what Augustine contributed to this ongoing Trinitarian theology was ground breaking and invaluable. Let us now turn to how the first Christian thinkers imagined and consequently explained the mystery of the Triune Life of God.

Trinitarian thought before Augustine

One of the more noticeable features of Christianity was the baptismal rite, celebrated "In the name of the Father, Son, and Holy Spirit" (Mt 28:19). This dominical mandate was performed ritually surely before it was understood theologically. Absent from the Christian scriptures, the term Trinity does not surface in the history of theology until Theophilus of Antioch (c. 115–85), who coined the Greek term τριάς to explain how the varied manifestations of creation could come from the one God while also each day showing forth the Trinity's personal distinctions. Theophilus thus argued that the first three

---

[9] *Trin.* 6.4.6; CCL 50.234.

days of creation are faint reflections of the three persons of the one true God named together at the end of Matthew's Gospel: "In like manner also the three days which were before the luminaries, are types of the Trinity, of God, and of his Word, and of his Wisdom. And the fourth is the type of man, who needs light, that so there may be God, the Word, wisdom, and man."[10] Notice how the first Christian usage of Trinity explicates both (1) the distinct three divine persons within the Godhead, as well as (2) the glory of the human person who is the earthly icon and similitude of the Triune God in heaven. As we shall see, this link was also central to how Augustine conceived of the Trinity, associating the beauty of that triune love with the *imago Dei* who finds fulfillment only in union with Father, Son, and Holy Spirit.

The first generations of Christians knew that the seeds of their creedal teachings and liturgical practices were all somehow strewn throughout the pages of sacred scripture. It was up to them to devise the nomenclature that would begin to describe the reality. So, although Theophilus nowhere found the Greek term τριάς in the Bible, as the Latin Tertullian (d. c. 240) nowhere chanced upon *trinitas* a decade or so later, these forerunners of Trinitarian thought read the Church's scriptures in such a way that they encountered the Triune God all around. It was essential that this new encounter not offend the Hebraic insistence on the monotheism upon which this new Christian truth is built—"Hear, O Israel! The Lord is our God, the Lord alone!" (Dt 6:4). Whereas the God of Israel is always and everywhere one, early Christian readers of these sacred pages described suggestions that this one God might also be three persons. Abraham's three visitors, for example, at Genesis 18, hint at how this singular "Lord" comes to be revealed in three distinct persons: "The Lord appeared to Abraham by the oak of Mamre, as he sat in the entrance of his tent, while the day was growing hot. Looking up, he saw three men standing near him. When he saw them, he ran from the entrance of the tent to greet them" (Gen 18:1–2). As the singular "Lord" unfolds into the plural "three," Genesis suggests that perhaps the one who has come to visit his people is in fact a trinity of persons. When Christians read the Prophet Isaiah's depiction of the heavenly act of angelic praise, "Holy, Holy, Holy" (Is 6:3), they again encountered a trinity of sorts, three simultaneous shouts of praise indicating three co-worthy of adoration.

This way of reading scripture and the Church's teaching continued in the next generation of theologians to think deeply on the Trinity, the second-

---

[10]Theophilus of Antioch, *Apologia ad Autolycum* 2.15; trans., Dods, Ante-Nicene Fathers, vol. 2 (Peabody, MA: Hendrickson Publishers [1885] 1995) 101.

century Apologists. Passionate Churchmen like Justin (d. 165), his student Tatian (d. c. 180), and Athenagoras of Athens (d. c. 190) needed to convince their hostile neighbors that Christians held onto an uncontested Monotheism while also worshipping the newly revealed Messiah Jesus Christ. If we take Justin as representative, we see how an obvious ranking of persons was present throughout these inchoate Trinitarian explanations. For without the later formulations of one substance, three coequal and co-divine persons, it was perhaps inevitable that the first minds to apply themselves to the Trinity would think of the Father as "first," the Son "second," and the Spirit "third."

In tracing this particular history, we should not cast suspicion on early representations of the divinity of the Son and the Holy Spirit, but instead show how such thinkers like Justin struggled to communicate terms and images with which he was able to keep all three persons equal in eternity and identical in divinity, while also upholding real personal distinctions. What is illuminating is that until Augustine, theologians lacked a rigorous and relational metaphysic that allowed them to depict the Trinity as three equally divine persons who differed not in essence but only in affiliation with one another. The tendency of most second and third century thinkers was to present the Son of God as one who possesses a divine nature somehow lesser than that of the Father's, as these early theologians relied on various labels to distinguish the Christ from the one true God—a second god, or an angel sent by the Father.

Justin is somewhat typical in his depiction here, ranking the persons of the Godhead so as to ensure that the true God remains unchangeable, indivisible, and eternal:

> We shall prove that we worship Him with reason, since we have learned that He is the Son of the living God Himself, and believe Him to be in the second place, and the Prophetic Spirit in the third. For this they accuse us of madness, saying that we attribute to a crucified man a place second to the unchangeable and eternal God, the Creator of all things, but they are ignorant of the mystery which lies herein. To this mystery we entreat you to give your attention, while we explain it to you.[11]

Positing the Father as the origin of all, the Son as he who breaks into the created order, and the Spirit who continues to prophecy in his Church,

---

[11]Justin Martyr, *First Apology* §13; trans., Thomas B. Falls, *St. Justin Martyr*, in the *Fathers of the Church Series*, no. 6 (Washington, DC: Catholic University of America Press [1948] 2008) 46.

Justin is representative of these second and third century thinkers who were unable to avoid subordinating tendencies and images that appeared to gradate the divine persons of the Trinity.

Such gradation did not only haunt the early Greek mind, but the first Latin theologian Tertullian also fell into the same pattern as he set out to show the interrelationality of the Father, Son, and Spirit. As much as he desired to stress their equality by giving each a place within the Godhead, Tertullian inevitably relied upon crudely material imagery that only reinforced a certain subordinationism; in trying to hold onto the divine unity, Tertullian employs images of outward organic growth, the tree extending upward from its roots, the headwaters giving way to the river. These images were certainly meant to emphasize the divine unity, that the persons of the Trinity were all surely God. But in so doing, the Trinitarian problems become obvious.

In choosing the Greek word προβολή, that which comes organically out of its source without break or degradation (thus oftentimes translated as an emanation or extension), for the Son and Spirit, Tertullian thinks he has come upon an apt description for the Son's begottenness from the Father, but has only furthered the ante-Nicene predisposition to subordinating each person: "For these are προβολαί, *or emanations*, of the substances from which they proceed. I should not hesitate, indeed, to call the tree the son or offspring of the root, and the river of the fountain, and the ray of the sun; because every original source is a parent, and everything which issues from the origin is an offspring." From this parent and offspring model, Tertullian deduces a natural third component, thereby illustrating his desired Trinity:

> For the root and the tree are distinctly two things, but correlatively joined (*coniunctae*); the fountain and the river are also two forms, but indivisible (*indiuisae*); so likewise the sun and the ray are two forms, but coherent ones (*cohaerentes*). Everything which proceeds from something else must need be second to that from which it proceeds, without being on that account separated. Where, however, there is a second, there must be two; and where there is a third, there must be three. Now the Spirit indeed is third from God and the Son; just as the fruit of the tree is third from the root, or as the stream out of the river is third from the fountain, or as the apex of the ray is third from the sun.[12]

---

[12]Tertullian, *Adversus Praexean* 8; trans., Holmes, as in Ante-Nicene Fathers, vol. 3 (Peabody, MA: Hendrickson Publishers [1885] 1995) 603; CCL 2.1168.

In combatting any suggestion of tritheism, Tertullian stresses the inextricable and inherent unity between persons. While keeping the indivisibility of the Monarchy supreme, as found in Justin's Trinitarian thought, the Son is deemed "second" and the Spirit "third." Furthermore, in this delineation of persons, we are given an image of descending divinity: as the roots give way to the tree, the river pours out into the fountain, and from the sun drops away the ray of light. While it is true that the same wood, the same water, and the same light are instantiated in each component of these analogies, each also represents the prior and more perfect principle on a lower, diluted level.

The impact of the most prolific and productive theologian of the ante-Nicene period, Origen of Alexandria (d. c. 254) is nearly impossible to appreciate. Despite his brilliant contributions, however, he was similarly unable to explicate the Trinitarian life sufficiently, failing to distinguish the eternal begetting of the perfect *imago Patris* from the creation of other *imagines Dei*. Eager to profess the scriptures and creeds in a manner consistent with the developing mind of the Church, Origen understood the Trinity to be a "threefold cord" from which the Church and all Christian living "hangs and by which it is sustained."[13] For Origen, the Triune life of God was central to his overall theology, and in the construction of this Trinitarian essentialism, he anticipated much of the Trinitarian doctrine taught by the later Cappadocian Fathers—namely, that Jesus's Incarnation is the key to understanding the inner life of the Godhead, and that this inner life is best described as *mia ousia, treis hypostases*—one substance, three persons—a neo-Nicene formula professed at the Council of Alexandria in 362 which, according to Christoph Markschies, is "fundamentally based on Origen's thinking."[14] As close as Origen may therefore be to the later orthodox position, we see him also struggle to keep each of the three persons equally divine.

Origen rejected what would become the Nicene byword *homoousios* as overly materialistic (and a term he knew was popular with the Modalists), a move that would contribute to his tarnishing reputation in later centuries, after the term is canonized in 325. He apparently found in the term a dangerous image connoting an unchristian conception of emanation or the distention of a substance. This compelled him to describe the Son as a

---

[13]*Homily on Exodus* 9.3; trans., Ronald E. Heine, *Origen: Homilies on Genesis and Exodus*, in the *Fathers of the Church Series*, no. 71 (Washington, DC: Catholic University of America Press, 1981) 339.

[14]"Trinitarianism," *The Westminster Handbook to Origen*, ed., John McGuckin (Louisville, KY: Westminster John Knox Press, 2004) 207–9; 207.

"second god" (δεύτερος θεός), holding in abeyance any accusations from the pagan philosophers that a co-divine Son would inevitably bifurcate the Godhead: "Therefore, though we may call him a second God, it should be understood by this that we do not mean anything except the virtue which includes all virtues, and the Logos which includes every logos ..."[15] While a careful thinker should refuse to hold a speculative theologian like Origen to standards to be worked out only later, I do want to illustrate how he struggled to describe the divine persons of the Blessed Trinity without falling into imagery and language suggesting a sort of subordinationism. For it would be up to Augustine in many ways to reconceive of the Trinity in a way that instantly and simultaneously evokes the equality of the divine persons.

Between Origen and Augustine are found Hilary of Poitiers as well as the Cappadocian Fathers, not to mention the two ecumenical councils that worked out the now canonically sanctioned formulae for conceiving of the Trinity. Hilary is the one theologian of the Trinity explicitly mentioned by Augustine (occurring at *Trin.* 6.11) where the Bishop of Hippo thanks the Bishop of Poitiers for teaching him how the distinction of persons can be delineated by divine attributes unique to each particular person. As Augustine informs us, someone who wished to put in a nutshell the special properties of each of the persons in the Trinity wrote, "Eternity in the Father, form in the image, use in the gift." He was a man of no small authority in the interpretation of the scriptures and the defense of the faith—it was Hilary who wrote this in his book on the subject.[16] The book in question is Hilary's twelve-book *De Trinitate*. In this pro-Nicene defense of the Trinity, Hilary works through the most common errors regarding the personal relationships between the Father, Son, and Holy Spirit.

The extremes of such common errors fell between the modalism of the Sabellians, on the one hand, and the subordinationism of the Arians on the other. While the early biographical details of Sabellius are minimal, we know that by the early third century he was in Rome popularizing a position of thought which taught that the Father, the Son, and the Holy Spirit were really three varying modes of the one divine God. These three manifestations

---

[15]*Contra Celsum* 5.39; trans., Henry Chadwick, *Origen: Contra Celsum* (Cambridge: Cambridge University Press [1953] 1980) 296; see also *Contra Celsum* 6.61 and 7.57. For a brief history of how Origen's Trinitarian theology played out in late antiquity, see Ilaria L.E. Ramelli's, "Origen's Anti-Subordinationism and its Heritage in the Nicene and Cappadocian Line," *Vigiliae Christianae* 65:1 (2011) 21–49.

[16]*Trin.* 6.11; Hill, *The Trinity* (I/5) 212–13; the text quoted here comes from Hilary, *De Trinitate* 2.1: *Aeternitas in Patre, species in imagine, usus in munere*; *Patrologia Latina* 10.51A.

occur in the soul of the creature and are not actually distinct persons in the Godhead. The worry on the other side of properly formulating a Trinitarian theology was that of the Alexandrian presbyter Arius who feared that defining the Son as *homoousios* with the Father bordered on ditheism—two gods of equal divinity. Arius instead preached a Christ who was one of like substance (*homoi-ousios*) to the Father, safeguarding the transcendence and unity of the Godhead. Hilary therefore finds himself caught between these two extremes: "if I oppose Sabellius (and define God's nature as three actually distinct persons), deny the one God and acknowledge the Son of God as the true God, a new heresy (viz., Arius') is ready to accuse me of teaching that there are two gods."[17] In fighting the Scylla of Modalism and the Charybdis of Arianism, Hilary is helpful in setting the parameters of the problem. However, distinguishing each divine person only by way of personal attributes is not really to offer a satisfying answer, Hilary in the end "contributing little or nothing to a solution," in the words of Edmund Hill.[18]

The solution's real beginnings must be traced back to the Church's first two ecumenical councils: Nicaea in 325 and First Constantinople in 381. While both councils shied away from illuminating how precisely the three divine persons were related within the one and same Godhead, both councils were more than clear that Father, Son, and Holy Spirit are each fully divine and each therefore equally worthy of adoration and worship. Both councils had to combat the subordination of the two originated divine persons, the begotten Son was rehabilitated at Nicaea against the Arians, and the Holy Spirit was acknowledged as equally κύριος at Constantinople. These conciliar deliberations laid the groundwork for proper theological discourse regarding each person of the Trinity.

Arius (d. 336), pastor of the Christians in the very important Baucalis region of Alexandria, wanted to ensure God's unity and transcendence by mitigating the Son's divinity, but he was met by clearer thought at Nicaea. Macedonius (d. after 360), Bishop of Constantinople, and his followers, the Pneumatomachi (literally, the "Spirit fighters") argued against the perfect divinity of the Holy Spirit on the basis of Heb 1:14 that teaches all ministering spirits are really gradated angels, the Spirit being the utmost of these blessed messengers. They were met by the collective thought of the Cappadocian Fathers and the magisterial decrees of the First Council of Constantinople.

---

[17]Hilary, *De Trinitate* 7.3; trans., Stephen McKenna, C.Ss.R, *The Trinity* in the *Fathers of the Church Series*, no. 25 (Washington, DC: Catholic University of America Press, 1954) 226.
[18]Edmund Hill, "Introduction," in *The Trinity* (I/5) 44.

Around 150 Greek-speaking bishops gathered at Constantinople in 381 to reaffirm both the core teachings of Nicaea as well as the condemnation against Arius, but also to censure the many-headed hydra which had sprouted since Arius's condemnation in 325—extreme Arians, the Anomoeans (or Heterousians) who wanted to declare the Son and Father to be of competing substances, the Homoeans or Acacians who wanted simply to affirm that the Son and Father were similar, and the Macedonians who wanted to apply the same disunity to the Holy Spirit.

The final crucial stage of Trinitarian theology before Augustine is found in the writings of the three great Cappadocian Fathers: Basil the Great (d. 379), his brother Gregory of Nyssa (d. 395), and their dear friend Gregory of Nazianzus (d. 390). Together these three theologians helped implement the mind of Nicaea and Constantinople, while forging what today is known as the "Cappadocian Formula"—namely, that God of Jesus Christ is to be understood essentially as *mia ousia, treis hypostases*. This formula of "*one substance, three persons*" gave the Church a foothold on which to advance Trinitarian speculation. This now set the parameters: one divine nature shared perfectly and without any hint of discriminatory subordination among three persons: Father, Son, and Holy Spirit.

Augustine's great contribution: Divine relationality

After three centuries of stops and starts, settlements and strife, what does Augustine of Hippo contribute to this legacy? Very early on in his intellectual life, Augustine shows great interest in understanding the triune life of God rightly; he sees triads everywhere he looks and deduces God's triune life active in every existent.[19] Among the first intellectual shifts that had to occur in Augustine's mind was the need to overcome the fallacy of Manichean dualism. This schizophrenic creed of two equally powerful deities, one good and one evil, for a time forced Augustine to imagine divinity as penetrable and thus material (however ethereally fine) as well as the things around him as somehow metaphysically suspect. But in coming to see God as one wholly good, and all of creation as divinely intended and therefore ontologically

---

[19]Such triads are indiscriminately described by Augustine as: *esse, essentia, manentia* (*ep.* 11.3), or *mensura, numerus,* and *pondus* (*conf.* 5.4.7; *Trin.* 3.9.18), or *mensura, numerus, modus* (*Gn. litt.* 4.3), *modus, species, ordo* (*ciu. Dei* 11.15: *c. Faust.* 21.6), or *unitas, species,* and *ordo* (*Trin.* 6.10.12).

beautiful, Augustine admits to achieving a certain sanity, realizing he is no longer compelled to live under the dread of two hostile deities battling it out on earth.

Yet the unity of God for Augustine is understood through the relationships that unify the three divine persons into perfect concord. Augustine's shorthanded formulation is telling: he recasts 1 Jn 4:8 and that *Deus Caritas est* into a Trinitarian framework: God is love, and wherever you see love, you see a Trinity.[20] This Trinity is what he will explore in his classic *De Trinitate*, which he began around 400 and did not complete it until two decades later.[21] *On the Trinity* still stands as one of the most significant reflections on the drama of God's inner life, and while scholars agree that Augustine was rarely without some form of Homoean heresy in mind, unlike other patristic treatises, his work on the Trinity "is less dominated than the writings of Athanasius and the Cappadocians by immediate polemics against the fourth-century heretics."[22] That is, with many of the Trinitarian heresies halted at Nicaea and I Constantinople, Augustine was liberated from having to contend with any one explicit enemy.

He was thus free to speculate more safely about the nature of God's Triune life. The result of such relative intellectual leisure was a work on the inner life of the Trinity which stressed an incredible relational dependence of each divine person. That is, unlike human persons who are autonomous and therefore accidentally related to one another only, each person of the Trinity is wholly and entirely reliant upon the other persons to be who he is as Father, or as Son, or as the Holy Spirit:

> But now it is not one thing that makes him great and another that makes him God; what makes him great is what makes him God, because for him it is not one thing to be great and another to be God; so it will follow, presumably, that the Father is not God taken singly, but only with and taken together with the godhead he has begotten; and so the Son will be the godhead of the Father ... And furthermore, because it is not one thing for him to be and another for him to be God, it follows that the Son will also be the being of the Father, just as

---

[20] *Trin.* 8.8.12: "... *immo uero uides trinitatem, si caritatem uides immo uero.*"; CCL 50.287.

[21] The reliable Pierre-Marie Hombert provides the year 422 when Augustine finally finished the *De Trinitate*; see his *Nouvelles recherches de chronologie augustinienne* (Paris: Institut d'Études augustiniennes, 2000) 45–80.

[22] Yves Congar, OP, *I Believe in the Holy Spirit*, trans., David Smith, vol. III (New York: Crossroad Publishing [1979–80] 1997) 80.

he is his Word and his image. This means that apart from being Father, the Father is nothing but what the Son is for him. It is clear, of course, that he is only called Father because he has a Son, since he is called Father not with reference to himself but with reference to the Son.[23]

When Augustine insists that there are not two factors in God, one causing him to be great and the other causing him to be God, he is eliminating the possibility of any accidental attributes in the divine nature. However, to deny accidents in God is not to be forced to predicate everything about God by way of substance. For there are realities within the Godhead that are predicated *ad aliquid*, with respect to the other wholly and essentially.

These are the "substantial relationships" which found no explicit expression in earlier Trinitarian conceptions of divinity, because all relationships were understood to be necessarily accidental and thus modifying to what a thing is.[24] But Augustine came to see that divine relations cannot by definition be accidental or altering: relationships are accidental only for mutable existents, so, if there is to be found a *relation* within the Godhead, it would have to be predicated *ad substantiam*. Here an Augustinian doctrine of divine simplicity emerges: it is one and the same thing to predicate an attribute of God *ad se* as well as *ad aliquid*. However, "although being Father is different from being Son, there is no difference of substance, because they are not called these things substance-wise but relationship-wise; and yet this relationship is not a modification, because it is not changeable."[25] The relationships within the Godhead can be said only with reference to another, thereby rendering the entire identity of each divine person other-centered. Unlike a human father, say, who exists substantially the same before as well as after the conception of his firstborn, God the Father is wholly and entirely dependent upon his Son to be who he is as Father. The Son, too, is utterly and fully dependent upon his Father to be who he is as the Begotten One; and the Holy Spirit relies on both to be who he substantially is as the Love between the Lover and the Beloved: "So the Holy Spirit is something common to Father and Son, whatever it is, or is their very commonness or communion, consubstantial and coeternal. Call this friendship, if it helps, but a better word for it is charity. And this too is substance because God is substance, and God is charity" (1 Jn 4:8, 16).[26]

---

[23]Trin. 7.1; Hill, *The Trinity* (I/5) 218.
[24]For an in-depth explanation of this, see Louis F. Ladaria, *The Living and True God: The Mystery of the Trinity* (New York: Convivium Press, 2010) 291.
[25]Trin. 5.6; Hill, *The Trinity* (I/5) 192.
[26]Trin. 6.5.7; Hill, *The Trinity* (I/5) 209.

This breakthrough in Trinitarian thought, that each divine person is wholly and inescapably an other-centered gift, challenges our contemporary understanding of divinity and perfection. Most today would equate perfection in terms of aloofness and autonomy. For instance, the wealthier I am, the less I need assistance. The more proficient I become at a task or skill, the less I need help or guidance. Yet, when the Son of God instructs his followers to be perfect as his heavenly Father is perfect (Mt 5:48), perhaps he is calling each of us to more vulnerability, calling us to more intimacy and recognition of how in fact we do need one another. From this understanding of each divine person of the Trinity being a substantial relationship wholly reliant upon the other two to be who they are as Father, Son, or Holy Spirit, any modern sensibility of perfection is surely challenged. In Augustine's pastoral care, perfection for the Christian does not necessitate flawlessness and impeccability (which in us creatures tends to foster a cold rigidity more than anything Christlike), but a warm receptivity of one's Savior. The American Capuchin theologian, Fr. Thomas Weinandy, OFM-Cap., has seen this paradox, splendidly arguing that:

> For human beings not to be completely constituted by their relationships may first appear to be a good thing. Human persons possess an independent integrity apart from their relationships. However, it is precisely this independent integrity which does not allow a human person to be given completely to another, but he or she must do so only through mediating words and actions, which express only a partial giving of oneself ... The persons of the Trinity are eternally constituted in their own singular identity only in relation to one another, and thus they subsist as who they are only within their mutual relationships. In their relationships to one another each person of the Trinity subsistently defines, and is equally subsistently defined by, the other persons.[27]

Weinandy expresses Augustine's connection between God and the human person perfectly: whereas the three divine persons are eternally and perfectly loving as mutual gift, the human person is made to be so. Unlike the Father, Son, and Spirit, however, we creatures are poised between the God who wills us into being and the nothingness from which we come. Our lives thus teeter between the divine invitation to surrender to the Love in

---

[27]Thomas Weinandy, OFM-Cap., *Does God Suffer?* (Notre Dame, IN: University of Notre Dame Press, 2000) 117.

whose image and likeness we have been created, and the selfishness which is the possibility of any created *imago Dei*. As creatures endowed with free will, we have a role to play in God's saving plan, or as the Bishop of Hippo preached at the shrine of the great Carthaginian martyr St. Cyprian (around 416), "You didn't, after all, give any consent to God making you ... So while he made you without you, he doesn't justify you without you."[28] But what is this *consensum* Augustine expects his people to cultivate? What does it mean to image the God who desired each of us and how is that image and likeness brought to perfection?

The human person as an image of the triune love

At the core, Augustine's understanding of the human person is a creature made for communion. Alone, a fallen soul has only distortion and disappointment. That is because an *imago Dei* is inextricably "hard wired" to find him or herself in another. But who is the other able to fulfill each of us? Who is able to quiet the restless heart? While never neglecting the necessity of creaturely community for human flourishing, Augustine knows from years of his own errant wanderings that just as each person of the Trinity enjoys his identity in the other, the same triune community of love is the only relationship that can complete the human creature. Gen 1:26 clues him into this: God forms created persons for the same community ("Let us ...") and for the same God ("in our image, after our likeness"). No creature can fulfill the *cor inquietum*, because every heart is made to find itself in the divine. Never one to leave a point of doctrine unexplored, however, one of the first Christian questions Augustine came to ask about the human person's being made in God's own image was fitting: What exactly is an *imago*?

From his immersion in Platonic images and ideals, Augustine would have learned of the inherent propulsion an image possesses to become like the prototype from which it is derived.[29] Similarly, Augustine understands

---

[28]s. 169.13; Hill, *Sermons* (III/5) 231.

[29]Plato understood the visible order as a copy of its heavenly model (e.g., *Timaeus* 29a-b), and Plotinus equated unreality with the separation between individual existents as well as the division between particulars and the One; all things emanate from the One and they are therefore essentially "the One" on lower levels. In that going-forth is also a longing to return. For a more detailed explanation of this cosmic return in which things become their truest selves, see Gerald P. Boersma, *Augustine's Theology of Image: A Study in the Development of Pro-Nicene Theology* (Oxford: Oxford University Press, 2016) 145–59.

an image to be the kind of "copy" that longs to become its prototype. Unlike something which simply looks similar to or is a duplicate of another, an image possesses an inherent propulsion to become that model from which it comes.[30] This appears early in Augustine's internal dialogue with the divine, captured in the *Soliloquia* (386–7). Admitting here how he wants to know nothing other than God and the soul, the *imago Dei* emerges as the nexus between the perfect Archetype and the derived duplicate. Let us eavesdrop on Augustine's [A] dialogue with Reason personified [R]:

> R: Does it not seem to you that your image in a mirror [*imago tua in speculo*] wants, in a way, to be you and is false because it is not?
>
> A: That certainly seems so.
>
> R: Do not all pictures and replicas of that kind and all artists' works of that type strive to be that in whose likeness they are made?
>
> A: I am completely convinced that they do.[31]

We hear in Augustine's soliloquy (a Latin term he himself invented) that it belongs to the nature of an image to strive to become the perfection upon which it is modeled. Alone, the image is not its truest self, suffering isolation and yearning to be completed by that for which it was brought into existence. Unlike a mere copy or some sort of doppelgänger, an *imago* is constituted not only by some similarity to a higher type, but also by its inescapable impetus to become ever more one with that Archetype.

In Augustine's Christian view of creation, then, all human persons are brought into existence to find themselves in living and transformative communion with the Triune God. And while he never denies that the human body shares in this divine imaging and likeness, evidenced by its heavenly upright posture, Augustine tends to locate the triune, divine image in the intellect first and foremost, *but only* when it is in union with the true Trinity from which it is derived.[32] So, the *imago Dei* is not simply the human soul's triadic makeup of memory, intellect, and will, which was so well worked out

---

[30]For more on this distinction and Augustine's early theology of *imago*, see *diu. qu.* 74. One of the classics on this point remains John Edward Sullivan, OP, *The Image of God: The Doctrine of St. Augustine and its Influence* (Dubuque, Iowa: Priory Press, 1963).

[31]*sol.* 2.9.17; Kim Paffenroth, *Soliloquies*, (II) 72–73; cf. *c. Acad.* 3.17.39.

[32]For those places where posture of the human body involves the *imago Dei*, see *Gn. adu. Man.* 1.17.27: "… even as a matter of fact even our body is so constructed that it indicates that we are better than the beasts and therefore more like God."; trans., Hill, *Genesis* (I/13) 57. See also: *Trin*: 12.1., *Gn. ad litt.* 6.12.22, *diu. qu.* 51.3.

in the latter part of Augustine's *De Trinitate*. To be an image of God is not simply to have the capacities of remembering, knowing, and loving. In truth, what it means to image God truly is to be in incessant union with God, epistemologically and ontologically. It is to be mindful of God in such wise that we begin to appropriate and thus share in that same divine life:

> This trinity of the mind is not really the image of God because the mind remembers and understands and loves itself, *but because* it is also able to remember and understand and love him by whom it was made. And when it does this it becomes wise. If it does not do it, then even though it remembers and understands and loves itself, it is foolish. Let it then remember its God to whose image it was made, and understand and love him. To put it in a word, let it worship the uncreated God (*colat Deum non factum*), by whom it was created with a capacity for him and able to share in him. In this way it will be wise not with its own light but by sharing in that supreme light, and it will reign in happiness where it reigns eternal.[33]

This is why the Augustinian *imago Dei* consists not merely in mental powers, as wonderful as such capacities are. This *imago Dei* in every created person is realized *because* "it is also able to remember and understand and love him by whom it was made." The true imaging of God consists in worship (*colat Deum*) as the memory, intellect, and will are actively raised in deifying union with the Triune God. The created trinity of memory, intellect, and will are therefore best understood not as static abilities to recall, know, and want. Instead, these are the ways the human person reaches out and adheres to the Father, Son, and Holy Spirit. In other words, Augustinian memory, intellect, and will are less powers as they are propulsions. These three mental components are thus activated entirely only as they reach out to the Triune God, fulfilled only when in transformative union with the Father, Son, and Holy Spirit who so lovingly created them.

The human person is thus created to worship and consequently grow in all the promises of the light and wisdom and joy of heaven. Such wisdom is transformative relationship; foolishness is isolation. Our author thus prays not to live his own life but to allow God to live his own divine life within Augustine's mortal and fragile frame. Apart from God, one can know only evil and purposelessness. Apart from remembering, knowing, and loving God,

---

[33] *Trin.* 14.12.15: Hill, *The Trinity* (I/5) 383; emphasis mine.

all other affiliations, as well as what we once considered a joy or a blessing will, in the end, prove transitory and temporary. God has created us in order that we allow ourselves to receive what he wants to give us, a participation in his very life. All is gift and the gift of God's self is hard wired into the human creature's being made in his own divine image and likeness. The priority of gift is always at the heart of any Augustinian doctrine, both ontologically as well as chronologically: ontologically, God's invitation and commitment to our salvation always outrace our own (e.g., *"interior intimo meo et superior summo meo"*[34]), and his grace always precedes our own agency.

It is important to stop and highlight the contemporary importance of Augustine's point here, that the human person is fully alive only in relationship outside of him or herself. Since we are made for covenant, for communion, we can never retreat within our walls of defensiveness. Other-centeredness is hence the core of Augustinian anthropology, but how often the Bishop of Hippo is blamed for modernity's solipsistic self. How many have blamed the author of the *Confessions* for introducing navel-gazing and an inordinate obsession to broadcast the deepest recesses of one's interior life to a wider public? Daniel Mendelsohn, for example, held up Augustine (and selected, in particular, the pear tree scene) as the one who began this modern fixation on the self. This "Augustinian preoccupation," as Mendelsohn calls it, put Western literature on the track of the overly introspective and narcissistic:

> It all started late one night in 371 A.D., in a dusty North African town miles from anywhere worth going, when a rowdy sixteen-year-old—the offspring of an interfaith marriage, with a history of bad behavior—stole some pears off a neighbor's tree. To all appearances, it was a pointless misdemeanor. The thief, as he ruefully recalled some thirty years later, was neither poor nor hungry, and the pears weren't all that appealing, anyway. He stole them, he realized, simply to be bad. "It was foul, and I loved it," he wrote. "I loved my own undoing."[35]

How responsible is Augustine for the Cartesian turn within? This is an important question in the age of "the selfie." From popular media like the *New Yorker* to more serious scholarship, many in the western intellectual tradition have seen Augustine as the forerunner to the modern turn within.

---

[34]*conf.* 3.6.11; CCL 27.33.
[35]Daniel Mendelsohn, "But Enough About Me: What Does the Popularity of Memoirs Tell Us About Ourselves?" *New Yorker* (January 25 , 2010) 68–74; 68.

While it is true that Augustine is responsible to a large degree for making the human soul the stage on which the eternal drama unfolds, the soul for Augustine is always actuated by reaching out and thus in union with the Triune God from whom and for whom it was originally made. The soul sins when it turns in on itself and perversely seeks itself as its own origin and goal. Confession is the only way out of this toxic turning in on the self, the *incuruatus in se*. In this, Augustine is clearly no forerunner to a modern Cartesian self thinking its own thoughts. In fact, Maurice Blondel (d. 1949) was so incensed by this connection being made in the French schools, he wrote: "Is there a contradiction more serious that the one that consists in finding his [St. Augustine's] influence in the Cartesian *cogito*? ... St. Augustine would never have dreamed of erecting his thought in 'rock,' of asserting himself as absolute in the absolute, of making the mind as we know it an isolable and sufficient substance."[36] The *mens* for Augustine is truly itself only in vibrant relation with the divine persons whom it images and for whom it has been created to become like.

The deified life is thus the goal of the human mind, the entire human person, turning toward the Triune God in order to bring the capacity to image and be like God to perfect fulfillment. This is what distances Augustine from any kind of Cartesian proclivities. In his excellent work on the use of Augustine today, Michael Hanby noted this well when he wrote:

> Augustine cannot be proto-Carteisan because the Augustinian self is only completed doxologically, by participation in the love and beauty of the Trinity through the mediation of Christ and his Body. This conviction is built into his very understanding of self-hood through an erotic, aesthetic conception of *uoluntas* and through the corresponding doxological constitution of the self manifest in the genre of confession. Already this is sufficient to distinguish Augustine from Descartes, but it does not go far enough in demonstrating just how far Descartes departs from and indeed inverts the position of his alleged forefather.[37]

---

[36]Maurice Blondel, "Le quinzième centenaire de la mort de saint Augustine (28 août 430)," *Revue de Métaphysique et de Morale* 4 (1930), as in *Dialogue avec les philosophes* (Paris: Aubier, 1966) 165, as in Jean-Luc Marion, "St. Augustine, or the Impossibility of Any Ego Cogito," *Augustine Our Contemporary: Examining the Self in Past and Present*, ed., Willemien Otten and Susan Schreiner (South Bend: Notre Dame University Press, 2018), 199–232; 203.

[37]Michael Hanby, *Augustine and Modernity* (London: Routledge Press, 2003) 161.

In communion with the one who brought him into being is Augustine's only chance at enjoying a life full of meaning and integrity, a life of purpose, and the gift of God's own self available at every moment. Divinization and doxology, this is the goal of every human life. For this we are made and for this the divided heart cries out for unity from without: "Let me not be my own life: evil was the life I lived of myself (*ex me*); I was death to me; but in you I began to live again."[38] Alone, Augustine knows he has only his sins. The only real truth he can claim wholly for himself is his own decay. All other realities are eternal relations: the charity for which he has been made, the true friendships that buoy his soul, the moments of joyful consolation, are all products of covenant, of being claimed by another for the sake of union. Only in "another" can one truly live again.

This is how Augustine's ecclesia so many centuries later can teach that the intimate dialogue between the Father and the Son reveals to humankind not only who God is but who the human person is to become as well. As Vatican II came to teach, when the Lord Jesus prayed his prayer of unity to the Father ("that all may be one … as we are one"; Jn 17:21–2), the Christ

> opened up vistas closed to human reason, for he implied a certain likeness between the union of the divine Persons, and the unity of God's sons and daughters … This likeness reveals that the human person, who is the only creature on earth which God willed for him or herself, cannot fully find him or herself except through a sincere gift of self.[39]

This is precisely Augustine's reality centuries earlier as well: a God who is a three-personed gift who brought about others made for the same other-centeredness, thus realizing one's own filiality before the Father as brothers and sisters of Christ Jesus. This familial incorporation assumes the freedom of the children of God who are desired for no other reason than for who they are. The dignity of the person is thus supreme: God brought all other creatures into existence for the sake of something else, but not man and woman. Whereas lower creatures have higher ends outside of themselves, human persons are ends in themselves. To maintain such an honor is not to excuse humans from dismissing all around them, but is meant to be a prompt

---

[38]*conf.* 12.9.10; Boulding, *Confessions* (I/1) 227.
[39]The Second Vatican Council's *Pastoral Constitution on the Church in the Modern World* (*Gaudium et Spes*) §24, slightly adjusted.

to show them that because they have been granted such self-possession, they must now come to flourish by fulfilling their God-given image and likeness, by surrendering to the grace which can make each gift. While there is no escaping our being made for God, this divine fulfillment is far from necessary. As gift, it cannot be forced. It must be freely opened, freely desired.

As "the only creature on earth which God willed for him or herself," the human person enjoys the sole status of having been brought about for no other reason than God's simply wanting to share his own life with those made uniquely in his image. Is this not love? How many of us would want to find out that we were indeed brought into existence for the sake of someone or something else? But since we are made as exceptional ends unto ourselves, we must find our truest self by giving ourselves away in lives of charity. That is, we shall never know who we truly are, creatures made for communion, until we surrender to the other-centeredness who is the Triune God. We can become ourselves only by gifting ourselves "in truth and charity." Only there can we "find ourselves" by imitating the Father, Son, and Spirit in allowing ourselves to become gift for the other.

This is the "joy and hope" of the modern world, resting on the organic unity of the human race that God willed for each of throughout all time by patterning our existence on his own. For ours is a unity foreshadowed by the Trinity, exemplified in the Incarnation, and intended for the Church still. As the Father is completely reliant upon his Son to be who he is as the Begetter, as the Second Person of the Trinity is wholly dependent upon the Father to be who he is as Son, and as the Holy Spirit is utterly reliant upon this eternal begetting as the love between them, the human person is similarly constituted and grows in charity as he or she grows to see his or her own self as a gift from and to the other. This is why any true life for Augustine is always collaborative. The human person, made in the *imago Dei*, is so constituted to become a gift for others in truth and in love.

Is it not true that you feel most alive when in communion with the other? It could be in the presence of a dear friend or simply sitting outside thanking the Lord for the beauties of nature. It often happens in a moment of helping another or tending to the needs of a child. We begin to realize that our flourishing is never about our own selves, but about ourselves in tender relationship with another. Even the solitary ascetic who seeks consecrated silence is instructed not to enter into *otium* so recklessly that he forgets the almsdeeds and the command to serve his neighbor. "No one ought to be so completely at leisure (*otiosus*) that in his leisure he takes no thought for serving his neighbor, nor should anyone be so fully active (*actuosus*) that he makes no room for the contemplation of God."[40] One goes into the desert not for oneself, not to escape the tumult of the world. One abandons a life in the world for no other reason than true communion and to serve, to find the Other more intently and thus intercede for the world he has left behind (and, conversely, one can never be so "in the world," that he or she does not practice some form of Christian prayer). In fact, Augustine's *Regula* (the *Rule* he composed to guide those in monastic life) opens with this encouragement: "In the first place—and this is the very reason for your being gathered together in one—you should live in the house in unity of spirit (Ps 67:7[68:6]) and you should have one soul and one heart (Acts 4:32) centered on God." There is no spiritual practice for Augustine that seeks to alienate or to foster separation, as even the strictest parts of this Augustinian Rule has directives on how to tend lovingly to the needs of the infirmed and the poor who seek solace.[41]

On the other hand, sin will always be understood as isolating and fragmenting, a self-imposed alienation from the community for which we have all been made. Sin in Augustine's view will always turn the self not only in *on the self*, but will inevitably turn the self *against the self*. As such, we are now ready to inquire into Augustine's understanding of human sin and the reasoning he provides on how, and why, free creatures can turn from the Go(o)d for whom they were made. We now turn to how our sinner-turned-saint understood the allure of evil. What is it we desire when we turn away from the one source who alone can fulfill our desires, who alone can still our restless hearts?

The young Augustine spent many years experimenting with all the possible ways we think that restlessness can be quieted. He sought over and over for that definitive relationship for which he had been made. How many of us have also worked our way through our worldly successes, material comforts, and human relationships only to look up one day and realize that we are still unsatisfied? Not yet satiated? This is the lesson Augustine came to see: we are made in the image and likeness of God and no other being—however wonderful—can truly satisfy. This was most poignantly learned in his life's story with the death of his friend in *conf.* 4. As we all do to various degrees, Augustine's young adulthood prized friendship above all other goods. When his friend died, Augustine thought there was no way he himself could continue—his absolute, his ultimate, had been taken from him, thus discovering how "wheresoever a human soul turns, it can but cling

---

[40]*ciu. Dei* 19.19; Babcock, *The City of God* (I/7) 376; CCL 47.686.
[41]See for example *reg.* 3.5, 5.5–11; this translation comes from *The Monastic Rules*; trans., Sr. Agatha Mary, S.P.B. (IV, 2004) 110.

to what brings sorrow unless it turns to you, cling though it may to beautiful things outside you and outside itself."[42]

Recognizing how Augustine had made his childhood friend from Thagaste the sweetness that surpassed any other sweetness he had ever known (*conf.* 4.4.7), he also came to recognize that no mortal could fill that role. He therefore admits to spending the ensuing days and weeks to finding only sorrow, walking only in darkness, finding his own native land a torment and all moments dreadfully odious. In these days of staggering and stupor, he "had become a great enigma" to himself (*Factus eram ipse mihi magna quaestio*), and struggles to go on.[43] As James Wetzel has so keenly observed,

> The terrifying prospect of Augustine's confessional logic is that love is an all-or-nothing affair. Either we love someone well and therefore in God, or we love a fiction of our interior poverty, a desperate projection of sin. Apart from God, in other words, we never get outside the fiction we take to be the self. It is only the vision of God as a redeemer who passes through death that diverts Augustine's logic from its all-or-nothing disjunction.[44]

Here begins the battle between God and self, the lesson in what constitutes my truest identity. The logic is that either I am made for God or I am only for myself. The latter results, as Augustine so viscerally came to feel, only in disappointment and despair; the former, however, fulfills the one relationship in which the human creature is to posit all other relationships. Only that love can fulfill and effect all others.

As Augustine journeyed through life, he infamously experimented with various pleasures in the hope of satiating his unquenchable self. His intellect outran all others and his heart bled to love and to be loved. It was not until he came to realize in whose image and likeness he had been made could he understood not only God's gratuitousness but the gravity of his own sin. His human romances ensnared him in lust, and his human pursuits of knowledge led him to pride. Yet in what would follow, he came to see that in Christ, love and knowledge were finally attainable and life giving. This is where he discovered what it meant to image God and eventually to become like him.

---

[42]*conf.* 4.10.15; Boulding, *Confessions* (I/1) 101.
[43]*conf.* 4.4.9; Boulding, *Confessions* (I/1) 97.
[44]James Wetzel, "Trappings of Woe," as in *Parting Knowledge: Essays after Augustine* (Eugene, OR: Cascade Books, 2013) 58–80; 79.

Conclusion

We began this work appreciating the rich contribution Augustine has made to helping Christians think rightly about the Trinity. Whereas the first generations of Christian theologians envisioned the Trinity in almost inescapably subordinationist terms, later thinkers like the Cappadocian Fathers and Hilary of Poitiers, labored to provide the Church with a more accurate theological taxonomy and imagery. In this development, Augustine's understanding of a *substantial relationship*, we were brought into the awesome mystery of the divine persons' need and reliance upon the other to be who they are. For the Father is entirely dependent upon his relationship with the Son in order to be Father; similarly, the Son is wholly needful upon the one who eternally begets in order to be Son, and the Holy Spirit is recognized only as the love between these two.

Because of this living from and for another, those made to the image and likeness of God should be aware of what their perfection consists. Instead of trying to amass a life for oneself, every human person must come to learn to live as a gift, as one made for relationship. The fullness of human flourishing, then, will consist in the proper ordering of one's loves, the proper ordering of making oneself gift. Made in God's own image and likeness, Adam and Eve were so constituted so as to find their fulfillment in and through one another. Neither was ever to make of the other an end in him or herself. Rather, they were to use all created goods in order to attain the Creator for whom they were made, who they were made to be like. Gazing upon the reality of the Trinity, humans should come to understand that the height of personhood consists in becoming wholly reliant upon a divine person. This is the Father; this is the Son; this is the Spirit who conjoins them eternally and perfectly. Yet for creatures to entrust themselves to another in imitation of their God requires a surrendering to grace, which is a risk each of us must take if we are ever going to understand who we truly are. Satan knew this step outward was required for Eden to become Paradise truly. The enemy knew that we humans have been created to allow another to enter our lives, and thus exploited our fears in no longer being the center of our own lives. He therefore promised that we could in reality become gods without God. This is the subject matter of our next chapter, continuing our foray into this divine drama and human persons' ability to find joy in God or misery in themselves.

CHAPTER 2
BECOMING GOD WITHOUT GOD?

"The moment you have a self at all, there is a possibility of putting yourself first
—wanting to be the centre—wanting to be God, in fact."

— C.S. Lewis[1]

We began our study into Augustine's understanding of self-loathing by first
uncovering his rich understanding of the Trinity as the eternal exchange of
love, three substantial relationships who are who they are as Father, Son, and
Holy Spirit because of their own mutual self-givenness and total reliance
upon the other. Here there is no withdrawal, no fear, no reluctance, but only
perfect rejoicing in the presence of another. Being wholly other-centered,
it was fitting that this Trinity bring about others made also for the sake of
self-gift: "Let us make human beings in our image, after our likeness" (Gen
1:26a). In this exhortative subjunctive, "Let us," Augustine descries a divine
deliberation wherein a Trinity of perfect persons freely brings about others
made to be like them and so find themselves by surrendering to love. In
making man and woman in his own image and after his likeness, God sets
this unique creature apart as the only being made for relationship, to find
oneself in another. As such, the human person, made as an echo of the
Trinity's own communal donation, is reflectively conditioned to find his or
her truest self also in a gift of self.

The human person was created to become one with God through
something not originally provided for in Eden, suggesting the drama of the
unfinished sixth day. Made wholly good, the human person was not made
wholly perfect. This is a crucial insight when understanding the drama of
human living as Augustine reads it unfolding in the opening chapters of
Genesis. As good as Eden was, there was something still to be received later
freely by creatures. Human persons were deliberately created with a free will
ordered toward the Good but also created with the demand that it be the

[1]C.S. Lewis, *Mere Christianity* (New York: HarperOne [1952] 1980) 49.

human person him or herself who surrenders to that Good. Or as Augustine would preach to his people, God naturally enough had to make you without you, but he refuses to save you without you: "... *fecit te sine te, non te iustificat sine te.*"[2] That is, each of us was created with a necessary role to play in the drama of our own salvation. Adam and Eve were created with a longing to which they were invited to surrender, made to discover that divine image and likeness and freely seek the one for whom they had been created all along. They had to receive this divine life intentionally and purposefully, to see how their excellence rested in God and not in themselves. This was the original foreshadowing of the age of grace, the coming of Christ. In abundance Adam and Eve enjoyed every natural good possible. Yet, they lacked the one supernatural thing, the one ultimate union, for which they were created—to become participatorily divine, the very promise Satan knew he could exploit.

This drama of Genesis begins, however, not in Eden but in the angelic realm. As a matter of appreciating the full narrative of Adam and Eve's fall, this chapter begins with a short section examining how Augustine understood the core components of Lucifer's. God the Father is the first to lose a son and in this angelic rebellion, we see how the original sinner and first beguiler (*primus peccator, primus preuaricator*)[3] turned away from the perfect Light in the fallen desire to find contentment with his own gloom. The devil and his followers were created as entirely good and joyous angels, but they chose their own imprisonment. The fallen angels rebelled against God's invitation to allow him to be their defining deity and instead sought divinity on their own. Seeking thereby to make themselves the ultimate reality, the devil becomes the first to invert the goods of creation. This is what Augustine understands to be the original concupiscence which continues to echo through every act of divine rebellion.

The second section telescopes downward into Adam's adventure as one also made for divine union. God orchestrated this creation beautifully and saw it most fitting that he create other free selves made in his own image and likeness. Tainted with absolutely no jealousy or envy, Augustine saw how apt it was that God freely allowed another order of existence into being.[4] Part of this new creation was endowed with God's own rationality and capacity

---

[2] *s.* 169.11.13; PL 38.923.

[3] *s.* 153.14; PL 38.832; *ep.* 105.4.13.

[4] Augustine could very well have read how Plato held that the Demiurge brought the visible world into existence because it is fitting that a good being, free from any jealousy (φθόνος), would bring other existents into being (*Timaeus* 29D–30A).

for communion, simply because God wanted to share his life in concord and in ecclesia. But why did God create angels who could fall away, and why did he not create men and women already in a state of unassailable blessedness? Why did he choose to create us in naturally perfect Eden but still just outside the supernatural doors of Heaven? God chose to create all persons good and oriented toward himself, but he refused to put them in an initial state of absolute beatitude without some sort of graced collaboration on their part. Provided with everything they required to remain in and even grow greater in their original state of beatitude, something was still required of their choosing, their desire to be wholly God's.

The third and final section assesses the major elements of Augustine's theology of sin. Here we summarize the elements of sin according to Augustine, rooted in the desire to become God without God (Gen 3:5). This is the pride that has severed the unity between Creator and creation, and Augustine understands how self-deification is a primal and persistent enticement which reverberates through every rebellion since. For Augustine, every sinful word, thought, or deed is an echo of Adam's turn away from God in an attempt to place himself at the center of all that is real. Think of a little child who wishes to disappear: he places his hands tightly over his eyes in the belief that if he cannot see you, you surely cannot see him. Behind his hands he hides, thinking that he has become invisible and thus impervious to interaction. This is Augustine's understanding of concupiscence: that fallen desire to be the determiner of what is real and of what is right and wrong.

Lucifer's leap

Contained in the *lux fiat* of the first act of creation (Gen 1:3),[5] Augustine sees in this initial blast of light something quite unique. Whatever is meant by the first creation of *lux*, it must be a type of light that precedes the creation of the sun and other celestial luminaries not brought about for three more days. Since God rested on the seventh day, all creatures

---

[5]While the light of Gen 1:3 is the first creature to be named by scripture, *lux fiat*, Augustine very cleverly reasoned that before anything could be created, the first reality to be brought about would not be a thing but the metaphysical factor of "being able to be brought into being." That is, before "light," there had to come the "ability to be formed into light," and to show this, Augustine coins the term *formabilitas* (at *Gn. litt.* 5.4) as that new metaphysical reality which is the foundation of God's creating *ad extra* as portrayed in the six days of Genesis.

must somehow be accounted for in the narrative of Genesis. That is why Augustine argues that the light of the first day is an incorporeal light and is in no way something that can be perceived by the senses. Unlike the physical lights brought into being on the fourth day, we learn that the light of the first day is actually angelic refulgence, an illumined participation in "eternal light which is itself the immutable wisdom of God." The first creatures are the hosts of angels whose luminosity is nothing other than the reflection of the Trinity's own brilliance, "since there is in them that light which was the first thing to be made."[6] In this way, Augustine makes it clear that angels were brought about in such wise that they were constituted to realize that it "is light not in himself but in God. If an angel turns away from God, he becomes unclean, as are all those who are called unclean spirits."[7] Such turning away is what the devil and his angels chose when they turned from the Uncreated Light with the result that God had to separate their self-imposed darkness from the participatory light which he had intentionally created. It is important to note this verbal change: God does not create the darkness, but he does allow it to go its own way, thus separating it from those angels who have instead chosen to remain in eternity and enjoy the certainty of blessedness.

This reading of Genesis achieves two aims for Augustine: first, it provides him with the scriptural warrant needed to explain the creation of angels, while it also establishes his clear anti-Manichean position that the first fall of sinful beings was not caused or intended by God, but was the matter of creatures' misusing of the otherwise good gift of free will. That is, if the angels are collectively represented by the *lux* of Gen 1:3a, the rebellious angels are captured in the darkness (*tenebras*) which God does not create but instead separates (*diuisit*) from that part of his creation which once clung closely to him. This diabolical "darkness" seems neither intended nor created, but God does allow it be separated if that is what Lucifer and his angels so choose.

Of course it need not have been this way. In Augustine's exegesis of Genesis, all created persons were designed to be able not to sin; all were created able not to die.[8] Yet this freedom was contingent upon clinging to

---

[6]*Gn. litt.* 2.17; Hill, *Genesis* (I/13) 200.

[7]*ciu. Dei* 11.9; Babcock, *City of God* (I/7) 10.

[8]Augustine of course distinguishes the goodness of Eden from the perfection of Heaven by cleverly stating that in the former we were *able not to sin* and *able not to die* (*posse non peccare, posse non mori*), while in heaven we are *not able to sin* and *not able to die* (*non posse peccare, non posse mori*); see *Gn. litt.* 6.25.

God aright: for God did not create anyone able to continue in the original creation without a subsequent choice to appropriate his invitation to perfection freely. True happiness necessarily involved proper worship. Unwilling to remain in this state of humble other-centeredness, the first one to fall from God did so in an attempt to live apart from a life of reliance upon another and praise of one higher. Yet even in this radical rebellion, Augustine sees how Satan still chose some sovereign. In fact, as we shall see, all sin is always a matter of choosing an ersatz deity. That is, made good and able to have remained good, Satan instead immediately chose not to remain one with the true Lord, but with himself only:

> So then the idea that the devil never stood in the truth, never led a blessed life with the angels, but fell from the very beginning of his creation, is *not* to be taken as meaning that he was created evil by the good God, not perverted by his own free choice … But the very moment he was made, he turned away from the light of truth, swollen with pride, and corrupted by delight in his own personal power. Thus he never tasted the sweetness of the blessed life of the angels. It is not that on receiving it he turned up his nose at it, but that by refusing to receive it he turned his back on it and let it slip through his fingers.[9]

Herein lies a shorthanded formula for all of Augustine's hamartiology, describing both the nature of the first and the essence of every sin thereafter: a pride that is puffed up and tumid (forms of *tumidus* being Augustine's most cherished adjective when describing what sin might look and feel like) which takes pleasure in its own power (*superbia tumidus, et propriae potestatis delectatione corruptus*). Sin occurs when a creature blessed with free will places a lower good over a higher, and the first account of this far-reaching inversion occurred when the devil placed his own self over God's self.

This primal act of overturning the proper order of charity is described as a swollen satisfaction and delight in one's autonomy. Augustine offers a lengthy analysis of this egocentrism, aided by the Holy Spirit when gazing into the power and allure of evil. The jealousy in question is of course *inuidia*, that looking (*uidere*) only at (*in-*) oneself because only oneself matters:

---

[9]*Gn. litt.* 11.23.30; Hill, *Genesis* (I/13) 445; emphasis added. At *ep.* 73.3 Augustine also wonders if the devil had ever been happy, a question for which he is asking for help.

In this work, however, our task is to inquire, in the light of holy scripture, what has to be said about the devil. In the first place, whether it was from the very beginning of creation that delighting in his own power he withdrew from that fellowship and charity which is bliss for the angels who enjoy God, or whether he himself too was for some time in the holy company of angels, equally just and enjoying equal bliss. Several authors say, you see, that what brought about his fall from the supernal regions was his jealous grudging of the man being made to the image of God. But against that is the fact that jealousy or envy comes after pride, not before it; jealousy after all does not cause pride, but pride does cause jealousy.

Since pride, then, is the love of one's own superiority, while jealousy is the hatred of another's good fortune, it is easy to see which comes from which. I mean, anyone in love with his own superiority will be jealous of his peers because they are treated as his equals, and of his inferiors in case they should become his equals, and of his superiors because he is not treated as their equal. Thus it is pride that makes people jealous, not jealousy that makes them proud.[10]

The proud person sees everyone as a threat to his or her own reign. In the traditional cataloging of the deadly sins, envy is just below pride because at least the envious person recognizes that he or she dwells in a state of lack, desiring something outside of themselves. But pride is disregard for all, and it is the sickness for Augustine, that malady from which flow all other disease. When the sinner feels threatened by another's goodness, jealousy arises and destruction inevitably manifests itself in some way—a hurtful action, unkind word, or even just an uncharitable thought of the other's unworthiness.

In the devil's case, he sees how men and women are like him, also made in the divine image. Sharing this unique relationship with creatures well below him is a clear challenge to his own uniqueness, unable to imagine a love that is not diminished when distributed. Having rejoiced in his angelic status, the enemy now becomes proud in thinking divine similitude was for him and his cohorts alone. However, such pride does not render Satan inherently evil. It causes him to lash out and thus lose his intimacy with his Creator but in stressing how the creation and the existence of the devil is ontologically good, Augustine has progressed far from his Manichean cosmology.

---

[10]*Gn litt.* 11.14.18; Hill, *Genesis* (I/13) 438.

In this truly Christian view, Satan is not the polar opposite of God. He is a forlorn son, a good creature who has unfortunately chosen to leave his Father's company but nonetheless remains eternally dependent upon God for his existence and agency. The cosmos finds itself not in a battle between two equal enemies. Instead, we are in a civil war filled with acts of patricide as a beloved son refuses to receive what his Father and God longs to give him:

> [Satan] too is not bad insofar as he is an angel but insofar as he has been perverted by his own will. One has to admit, you see, that angels too are changeable by nature, if God alone is unchanging. But, by that act of will by which they love God more than themselves, they remain firm and steady in him, and, in being most willingly subject to him alone, they enjoy his greatness. That angel, however, by loving himself more than God, refused to be subject to him, and thus swollen with pride, he deserted the supreme Being and fell. And because of this he is less than what he was, since he wished to enjoy what was less, when he wished to enjoy his own power more than God's.[11]

But why would a creature do such a thing? Could an angel at least not have seen the havoc and distress this would bring?[12] Augustine's answer lies in the paradoxical nature of pride: the proud person would rather embrace his or her own insufficiencies than blossom by entrusting themselves to another.

Augustine translates this act of angelic insurgence into what Satan extends into the Garden of Eden. In his rebellion, Satan wants to bring as many created persons with him in order that he may relish their sufferings as well: "This is what the devil is like: he wants to seduce people so that they may be punished with him. He tries to persuade us to sin in order to have real charges to press against us."[13] Augustine thus understands that there are two sources of sin, directly from the individual fallen will and indirectly through the persuasion of another, but the dynamics of sin remain the same.[14] For both with angels and with humans, we see creatures gifted with

---

[11]*uera rel.* 13.26; Hill, *True Religion* as in *On Christian Belief* (I/8) 45.

[12]In *ep.* 73.3.7, Augustine writes Jerome and asks him to help him understand Satan's initial mind. What Augustine wants to argue is that the devil was always good but never happy because he foresaw what he would do and how he would choose to live apart from the fullness of God; *lib. arb.* 3.9.25.

[13]*en. Ps.* 96.11; Boulding, *Expositions* (III/18) 449.

[14]See *lib. arb.* 3.10.29 for more on this distinction between Augustine's understanding of the "two sources of sin" (*duae origines peccatorum*)—one's own fallen will or the persuasion from another.

the ability to turn toward God permanently and freely or to turn away from him. Perhaps not as cosmic and simultaneously permanent, if humanity like the angels would have "participated equally in wisdom, they too would have continued in its eternity, they would have been equally blessed, because equally certain of their blessedness."[15] Like angelic persons, human persons were equally endowed with the summons to turn toward the divine fully and thereby never experience dissolution and despair. This invitation is best represented for Augustine by the Tree of the Knowledge of Good and Evil. Let us now turn toward the Adamic adventure as portrayed in the early chapters of Genesis. In this next section we shall accordingly concentrate on why God created Adam and Eve good, but incompletely. This reality is, for Augustine, marked by the fact that the first human persons are created on a day without end and the divine prohibition given them regarding the tree that was positioned in the middle of Eden.

Creation: Wholly good but incomplete

If any of the Church Fathers should appreciate the constancy of God, it would be the youthful and mercurial Augustine of Hippo. Only after decades of indecision, after years and years of trial and error, Augustine finally surrendered to the consoling truth of Christ. Perhaps it was this radical realization of God's providential patience that also gave him deep insights into the beauty of the opening verses of the Bible. For more than most early exegetes, he observes how there is something God respects about the slow unfolding of creation and the gradual nature of growth. Serious conversion demands time, and it is Augustine's God who created fruit that must ripen, newborn animals that have to grow up, and persons who have to mature. This bespeaks God's gentleness and even humility, for Augustine's God would rather risk some imperfection than ignore a created person's ability to develop freely, and in that process appropriate his or her own sense of divine collaboration and accomplishment. Augustine's world is a world ever in motion, guided by a loving Father who is always at work (cf. Jn 5:17), infused with latent causes of things still to come.

As we saw in our opening chapter, the human person and all creatures had to be (naturally enough) to be brought into existence by God without the creature's consent. God, however, had thus determined all along to

---

[15]*ciu. Dei* 11.11; Babcock, *City of God* (I/7) 13.

include the human creature's gift of free will in his own plan of salvation. A free, loving, three-personed God could not create computers or automata in his own image and likeness. Instead, God created other free persons, other selves who therefore inevitably had the option of making themselves primary. This is the adventure of human living, and according to Augustine this is why God did not create those made in his image and likeness already in the fullness of his presence. While he is very careful not to purport to know the cause of God's overall plan in his willingness to create, Augustine will venture to maintain that in creating, God simply wanted to share his bliss with others made to reflect his perfections. Yet this remains always an invite and never a demand. Augustine begins the story of the human race by emphasizing humanity's inherent goodness: divinely intended and desired by God, angels and humans are created essentially good with the ability never to offend God or one another. Such charity is however not automatic but has to be freely assimilated.

Augustine first descries humanity's incompleteness in his reading of Gen 1:31, that all things are deemed "exceedingly good" (*ualde bona*). Unlike the protological formula found for the other days of creation, "God saw that it was good … evening came, morning followed—the X day," Augustine appears to be the first in the Tradition to highlight the sixth day's open-endedness. Whereas days prior receive their own confirmation of completion and the explicit awareness that each day's morning came and its evening followed as directed, the day on which the human person is brought into being fails to receive its own stamp of conclusion. In Augustine's mind, it is a day left intentionally open, a day with more work to be done. So, when he read about the sixth day, he surmised how the human person was of course created good but not complete. That is, the day on which Adam and Eve are created ends with the author of Genesis relaying that "all things (*cuncta*), whatsoever he made to be very good" (Gen 1:31).

Cosmogony prepares one's anthropology, and Augustine's Genesis commentaries against the Manicheans defend not only the unity of the Godhead but the communion for which the human person has been brought into being. Stressing Adam and Eve as the primal image for Christ and his Church, Augustine then looks at God's purpose in pointing out that it is not good that the man be alone (cf., Gen 2:18). His answer is not only ecclesial and the nuptial union which makes up the Church, the Bridegroom, and the Bride, but also an existential insight into the fact that Adam, although made good, is incomplete because, "there still remained, after all, something for him to become (*adhuc enim erat, quod fieret*)."[16] While he does not expound on this point, we know from later works that Augustine locates the foreshadowing of the Son of God's Incarnation, following St. Paul in Romans 5, in the First Adam. What is important for our purposes in this present chapter is to see how our author wants to maintain that both Adam and Eve were naturally good but supernaturally incomplete. There remained something for them still to do, namely, freely choose to orient their will wholly and eternally to the surrender of the Triune God.

Immediately after ordination to the priesthood, Augustine again takes up another Genesis commentary, albeit one he would never complete, the *Unfinished Literal Commentary*. Here he treats Gen 1:31 only once, and that is to argue for an understanding of evil as a *priuatio boni*. Since all things (*cuncta*) are very good, evil cannot be a thing but must be the absence thereof, a watershed insight Augustine learned while in the Milanese Neoplatonic circles. Whereas during his Manichean phase he located evil in the nature of all things, the *libri Platonicorum* taught him that evil could not be located in subhuman things, but in the assertion of a free self over all else: "Again, that all things that God made, however, are very good (Gen 1:31), while evil things are not part of nature, but everything that is called evil is either sin or the punishment of sin …"[17] As we saw in the *Refutation of the Manicheans* above, even though the first humans were not yet fully who they were made to be, this incompleteness does not render Adam and Eve anything less than good.

Many years later Augustine once more returns to these verses, and in his lengthiest commentary on Genesis, we read again how he continues to situate Adam and Eve in a good-but-not-yet-perfect state. The sixth day on which the human creature was brought into existence does not receive its own "and God saw that it was good, the sixth day." Instead, we hear that *all things* on this day are now declared good, and Augustine deduces this is because the human person is not ready to be declared good until his life's story surrenders to Goodness:

> Now did he not say individually the human creature, as in the other cases. *And God saw that it was good*, but after the man was made and given rights, whether to rule or to eat, he concluded about them all: *And God saw all the things that he had made, and behold they were very*

---

[16]*Gn. adu. Man.* 2.11.15; Hill, *Genesis* (I/13) 81.
[17]*Gn. litt. imp.* 1.3; Hill, *Genesis* (I/13) 115.

good. This is certainly a point that deserves investigation. They could, after all, have been paid individually the same respect as had been paid individually to the other thing that had been made before, and then finally it could have been said of all the things God made, *behold they were very good* ... Or was it because he was not yet completed (*perfectus nondum erat*), because not yet established in paradise—as if this "that" was left out here was said later on after he had been put there![18]

In noticing that the sixth day does not receive its own singular and separate ratification of goodness Augustine wonders why this day is not endorsed like the others. Whereas other days of creation end with the declaration that it is good and that "evening came, morning followed," and it seems that the other days enjoy a certain closure. Yet the one day, the sixth, on which created images and likenesses are made, fails to enjoy such conclusion. Moreover, instead of repeating the simple goodness of the other days, this sixth day is said to be "very good." Obviously something is different here; something unparalleled is brought into being at the end of the creation story. Augustine's solution? There is something still to be completed.

Clearly it is one thing to be good and another to be perfected. Unlike every other creature, supposedly, Adam is the only one made in this conditionality. Cheekily, G.K. Chesterton once quipped that a literary work entitled *A History of Cows* might leave a reader a bit wanting, coming in as "one of the simplest and briefest of standard works."[19] Unlike cows and other sub-human creatures, men and women possess a drama demanded by their own perfection. As a divinely intended creature, the highest visible creature in fact, Adam is no doubt good (*bonum*), but Augustine now wonders why he is created "not yet completed" (*perfectus nondum erat*). He is made for God and God alone can complete him. This is why Augustine's gloss here continues by way of New Adam typology. The first Adam's very being cries out for another. This is how we come to learn that Adam is the first only chronologically; existentially there is another who is prior because greater, the pattern upon whom all human flourishing is based. Even before he sins, Adam is not yet fully who he is meant to be. Why not? He must surrender; he

---

[18]*Gn. litt.* 3.24.36; Hill, *Genesis* (I/13) 239.
[19]G.K. Chesterton, "The Sun Worshipper," ch. 10 of *A Miscellany of Men* (Norfolk, VA: HIS Press [1912] 2004) 56–60; 56.

must choose to continue in that state of grace in which he has been placed. Again, Adam is free; he is no mere brute creature; his very being points to the Christ.

The man therefore before sin and in his own kind was of course good; but scripture forbore to say this, in order to say instead something that would foreshadow something yet to come. What was said about him, you see, was not untrue, because while someone who is good as an individual is clearly better when taken together with all the others he must also be good as an individual.[20]

Adam as an individual is of course "good," but he is clearly better when seen in communion with others. In fact, he is different from any other creature on earth. Adam is ruefully declared to be "alone" (Gen 2:18) and in need of the communion for which he has been brought into being.[21]

This is why the human race is created differently than the other animals who are brought into being in pairs. In Augustine's mind, the Adamic origin of the human race is a sign of our cohesion and community, signifying a bond that no other creature can enjoy:

> For this reason God wished to produce all persons out of one, so that they would be held together in their social relationships not only by similarity of race, but also by the bond of kinship. The first natural bond of human society, therefore, is that of husband and wife. God did not create them as separate individuals and bring them together as persons of a different race, but he created one from the other, making the side, from which the woman was taken and formed, a sign of the strength of their union. For those who walk together, and look ahead together to where they are walking, do so at each other's side.[22]

There is a beautiful tenderness here in Augustine's view of the marital bond: made in another's image and likeness, the human person is incomplete

---

[20] Gn. litt. 3.24.37; Hill, Genesis (I/13) 240.

[21] Augustine's usual way of explaining Gen 2:18 is how Eve is of course needed for the propagation of the human race (e.g., Gn. litt. 9.2.3), but also how she is an image of scientia, that part of the human soul which knows how to make its way in this world (Gn. adu. Man 2.11.15); for more on the latter, see my "Grata Sacris Angelis: Gender and the Imago Dei in Augustine's De Trinitate XII," American Catholic Philosophical Quarterly 74 (Winter 2000) 47–62.

[22] b. conjug., The Excellence of Marriage, Kearney (I/9) 33.

without personal communion. Unlike the other animals, God did not create the human race in already-established pairs, but brought all out of one man. As we have seen, the central point of this single origin has a key Christological importance (that all men and women are made for the God-made man), but Augustine also sees here an important lesson in the relationship between fidelity, love, free will, and our choosing to walk "together" with our eyes and heart on a common goal.

Eternally unifying love is a bond that can be neither implanted necessarily in creatures (the way brute animals "unite" only out of instinct), nor can it be externally enforced. It must be freely chosen, and that is why our author conflates our original sinlessness, our commonality as a human family, and the possibility of Eden's loss:

> For, while God created some animals that are solitary and, preferring solitude, keep to themselves ... he created others and would rather gather together and live in flocks ... But he did not propagate either of these kinds from single individuals ... Man, however, whose nature was in a manner to be intermediate between the angels and the beasts, God created in such a way that, if he submitted to his creator as his true Lord, and if he kept God's commandments in devout obedience, he would without dying obtain a blessed and unending immortality and pass over into the company of the angels; but, if he offended the Lord his God by using his free will proudly and disobediently, he would be given over to death and would live like the beasts.[23]

Charity and unity have always been synonymous in Augustine's mind and here on this cosmic level, we see how Adam's singular existence represents the radical communion intended for the entire human race. Even the "Mother of all the living" would come forth from the side of the first human, so as to stress how all humans are to find their truest selves collectively in the other.

Yet all of this depended on our free participation. Such surrender is realized in Augustine's frequent employment of *si*-clauses: only *if* we obeyed God, only *if* we would follow his ways. Love and communion cannot be forced, that is why the sixth day is different from all the other days. A story is still being written here. That is why God did not create humans in a pair

---

[23]*ciu. Dei* 12.22.21; Babcock, *City of God* (I/7) 62.

like the rest of earth's inhabitants, but created Adam in an original state of solitude. This is also why the sixth day remains "unfinished," thus pointing to another still to come. As sole origin, Adam thus represents the closeness the Creator intends for the human family. The result of this intended intimacy is that every human must come to understand him or herself as the reflection of another, of the very Goodness that brought them into being. It means to fight any temptation to fall back into oneself, the temptation to be oneself alone. To become an object for oneself, to take delight in one's own possible autonomy is the beginning of chaos. It is here all division and consequent destruction begins.

In Chapter 1 we learned how the human person is the only creature made in the divine image and likeness, the only creature made to find its truest self in the gift of another. But this is not all of course: the human person is also the only one to have also received a godly mandate. Adam is the only one whom God addresses directly in this wonderfully wild story of Genesis. All other creatures are left to fulfill their natures by being simply what they are. But those made like God are provided with what will prove to be a long series of commands of how to make their vocation to become divine a reality: "The Lord God gave the man this order: You are free to eat from any of the trees of the garden except the tree of knowledge of good and evil. From that tree you shall not eat; when you eat from it you shall die" (Gen 2:16–17). The Lord God honors the man by inviting him into a command, empowering him as an agent, as a participant in his own providence. What Augustine stresses when turning to this heavenly communication, it is not Adam's ability to follow God or not, but the apparently nebulous nature of the command itself.

What is it about this tree that cordons it off from the rest of the vegetation available to Adam's appetite? Why this fruit and not the others? Is the divine mandate so absolute that it stands in need of no justification or explanation whatsoever? Augustine's answer comes by way of his amazement that this command appears to be one that is not morally self-evident. It is not a precept that seems to be able to be deduced from natural powers or understood initially by the light of human reason alone. When examining this particular tree, Augustine quickly expresses pleasure (*placeat*) that no Christian exegete argues that the fruit of this tree is prohibited because it is inherently bad. That is a strictly Manichean position; but in the Christian world, all things are good and all things in Eden are very good. But why then is this tree off limits? Augustine is clear that this command comes not from a capricious and voluntaristic Deity. God has obviously made this tree to be the sort of tree that when violated has deleterious effects for humans. God has intentionally set this one tree in the middle of the garden, indicating that this is a tree endowed with a nature central to Edenic bliss—a tree that is made to be left alone, the sort of tree whose fruit one plucks only at one's own peril.

Think of the beautiful glistening leaves of the plant leadwort. These five-petaled leaves shine with blue in the summer and a fiery red come autumn. Neither botanist nor gardener would dare classify leadwort as an evil or detestable plant, but it will cause severe skin irritation if handled for any extended period of time. Perhaps there is an analogy here: the Tree of the Knowledge of Good and Evil is not intrinsically malicious but it is the sort of tree that the Creator made not to be touched by humankind. It was made for that purpose, and that is why it alone receives this name. It is not as if God looked around and for no particular reason, simply pointed and said, "that tree," but he clearly knew what picking the fruit of the Tree of the Knowledge of Good and Evil would do to a creature called to trust.

At this pivotal moment in salvation history, it is important to understand how Augustine stresses that God does not introduce Adam to discipleship by dictating something like "Do not take innocent life" or "Treat Eve as your only beloved." These are commands any rational person, especially any prelapsarian person, could surely figure out. What lies at the heart of the "you shall not eat" injunction is the trust to which God invites his divine images. So, it was not as if God gave a commandment that could be deduced by simple moral cogitation or by seeing the obvious and immediate implications of such a commandment. It is important to see Augustine's point here: God gives no command separate from his desire from an "I–Thou" relationship for which he had created men and women in the first place. In Augustine's view, God instead imposed an edict that in and of itself was wholly reasonable but not altogether self-evident, and this is how Augustine weaves filial trust and creaturely obedience into his exegesis of divine commands. God's laws are not simply about keeping oneself pure by following some inviolable code. God's ways are ultimately about the relationship and the intimacy only interpersonal trust can bring about. Even so, since there is something intrinsically different about the nature of this tree that sets it apart from the rest, Augustine avoids falling into any sort of fideism or irrationality.

Similarly, the location of this tree also distinguishes it from the rest of the trees in the garden. Situated in the middle, it is a standard bearer of God's desire to be at the center of our lives. If we keep God and his ways as the epicenter of how we orient our lives, we shall grow to become ever more like him. If we substitute him for ourselves, we shall seek godliness apart from its only possible source. This is why Augustine's earliest wrestling with Gen 3:5—"you shall be like gods"—is found in his particularly anti-Manichean commentary on Genesis, recasting this temptation into humanity's refusal to be under God but instead seek to live as their own masters without the Lord. Augustine sees in this a "jealous refusal" to trust that life in God would be more excellent and fruitful, than a life spent only under human powers and perceptions. In this, Adam and Eve became fond of their own power and they slowly became comfortable with the uncomfortable:

> wishing to be God's equals, to make bad use of that halfway centrality, represented by the fruit of the tree set in the middle of paradise, by which they were subject to God, and had their own bodies subject to themselves; to act, that is, against God's law, and so forfeit what they had received, while they had wanted to grab what they had not received. Human nature, you see, did not receive the power to enjoy the state of bliss independently of God's control, because only God is able to enjoy blessedness and bliss by his own power independently of anyone else's control.[24]

According to Augustine, what God was really after was not regulating Adam and Eve's diet, but desired to make clear to them that they were to live truly out of their trusting and the consequent obedience that flowed from living under a loving Lord. This is why he showed them what the center of their lives was to be, a manifest and clearly visible tree that stood for the life-giving fruit on which they were to feast abundantly.

To feast as God willed, however, meant also acknowledging that the tree was not their own. It was not of their planting but was wholly gift. Such a worldview would mean admitting that there was a God to whom one was indebted. The Tree of the Knowledge of Good and Evil also stood for the ordering of loves. It was the locus of proper praise, a sort of early sacramental worldview in which visible creatures were to raise one's eyes away from oneself and on to the Creator who longs to lavish his obedient creatures with all he has and is:

---

[24]*Gn. adu. Man.* 2.15.23; Hill, *Genesis* (I/13) 86.

Now it was necessary that the man, placed under God as his Lord and master, should be prohibited from doing something, so that obedience might itself be his virtue by which to deserve well of his master. This, I can indeed say with absolute truth, is the one and only virtue for every creature that is a rational agent under the authority of God, while the first and greatest vice, puffing it up to its own downfall, is the wish to assert its own authority (*sua potestate uelle*), the name of this vice being disobedience.[25]

Created in that state of good-but-not-yet-perfected, Augustine sees it most fitting that there be prohibitions and promises built into humanity's initial state. Obedience unto the Almighty is its own reward. Having been created in this divine image and likeness, humanity's protoparents had to trust that their ultimate satisfaction would be realized in a unifying and thus deifying union with God. Able to turn toward that God in the fulfillment of their nature, or away from him toward their own destruction, Adam and Eve are created in a state of invitation and trust which is made manifest in this one prohibition.

Such a command is also aimed at elevating the first man and woman to see that they would flourish in proportion to listening to their Creator and experience dissolution if they disobeyed. Augustine continues his Genesis commentary by next writing:

So the man then would have had no reason to reflect that he had a Lord and master (*sub Deo*), and to feel it in his bones, unless he had been given some order. And so that tree was not evil, but it was given the name of the knowledge of discerning good and evil, because if the man should eat of it after being forbidden to do so, there was in it the future transgression of the commandment, as a result of which the man would learn through his experience of the penalty what a difference there was between the good of obedience and the evil of disobedience.[26]

Sin, then, is the exact opposite of appropriating the divine life through reliant trust. It is to become one's own authority, one's own sovereign. Augustine therefore sees in the command not to eat of this tree, the possible

---

[25]*Gn. litt.* 8.6.12; Hill, *Genesis* (I/13) 354.
[26]*Gn. litt.* 8.6.12; Hill, *Genesis* (I/13) 354.

rebellion of those persons created with free choice. Such a choice determines a destiny, and the human race's invitation to eternal excellence hangs in the balance. Either we learn to surrender to God's will because we trust that it is better for us than our own desires apart from God, or we try to fulfill our divine image and likeness alone and apart from real divinity.

> Finally, the sinner was aiming at nothing else but not to be under God as his Lord and master, when he committed an act where the only reason to be attended to for not committing it was the command of his Lord and master. If this were all that was attended to, what else would he be attending to but God's will? What else but God's will would he be loving? What else but God's will would he be preferring to a human will? The Lord indeed will have seen why he gave the order; what he ordered is to be done by the servant, and then perhaps he too may deserve to see why the order was given. But still, to avoid spending any more time looking for the reason for this order, if serving God is in itself of great benefit to humanity, simply by giving an order God makes whatever he wishes to order beneficial; with him, surely, we never have to fear that he could order anything injurious.[27]

What is important is not the fruit itself, but the two parties involved in the directive about the fruit—the One who issued the command and the couple invited to follow it. The Creator's choice to put good-but-not-yet-perfected beings in Eden is not about forming subjects who mindlessly do what they are told, but rather to raise a people who have come to listen to the Lord simply because he is their only God.

Because such giftedness is invited and not enforced, the great story of God's people, God's City, begins. Here there are only free actors, other creatures brought into existence in order to enjoy concord and perfection. Made to cling to God, each in its own proper way, angels and human persons are at the center of this epic. Here is a drama poised between two extremes, the one perfect God and the *nihil* from which God brought all other beings. The lives of those endowed with free will thus teeter between the fullness of being and the utter nothingness from which they have come. As long as we freely turn to God and desire him as the center of our being, only happiness follows; if we choose to turn away, however, misery and incessant diminishment are freely ours as well. The ultimate blessing of human life,

---

[27]*Gn. litt.* 8.13.30; Hill, *Genesis* (I/13) 363–4.

therefore, is found in the free ability to turn toward God and find how deeply he made us for himself. This is the primal yearning of every human heart; it is the definitive telos by which we consciously or unconsciously make every other decision. We are made to become like God and nothing short of that deification will do. This is the glory of human living, but it is also the gamble, as we shall now see.

The metanarrative of Augustinian sin

We have so far seen that all classes of created persons, angelic and human, were created with a role to play in their own graced state of salvation. To this grace, the good angels responded instantly and eternally, while the rebellious angels had to be separated from that burst of light. Similarly, the first human parents were placed in a naturally perfect state in which they were able never to sin and therefore able never to die, but the choice was theirs to make. Because Adam was made for God but was not yet god, his will was susceptible to temptation. Jealous of his initial uprightness, Satan set out to tempt Adam away from the God whom Satan had just rejected. A fallen angelic mind, the enemy knew exactly whom, when, and how to strike.

In composing his *Spiritual Exercises*, the founder of the Jesuits, Ignatius of Loyola (1491–1556), likened the enemy of our human nature to a clever and cunning military strategist who would figure out the exact right spot to attack. Steeped in the world of late medieval chivalry and living his early life as a soldier and army commander, it is not surprising that Ignatius drew from his own lived experience in order to understand the workings of the spiritual realm. In describing the tactics of Satan, he warns those trying to advance in the ways of Christ and his Church that:

> The conduct of our enemy may also be compared to the tactics of a leader intent upon seizing and plundering a position he desires. A commander and leader of an army will encamp, explore the fortifications and defenses of the stronghold, and attack at the weakest point. In the same way, the enemy of our human nature investigates from every side all our virtues, theological, cardinal and moral. Where he finds the defenses of eternal salvation weakest and most deficient, there he attacks and tries to take us by storm.[28]

---

[28]St. Ignatius of Loyola, *Spiritual Exercises*, "Rules for the Discernment of Spirits" §327: trans., Louis Puhl, SJ, *The Spiritual Exercises of St. Ignatius* (Chicago: Loyola University Press, 1951) 146.

Whether it be that remaining piece of pizza for the glutton, the unfortunate encounter for the gossip already having a bad day, the scantily clad for the lustful teen, the enemy of our human nature knows how to elicit sin from the divided heart. But what do we see when we abstract from these particular sins? What is at play when we pull back from examining the virtues in particular as Ignatius does, and look at the metanarrative of sin? Augustine would no doubt agree with Ignatius that the enemy knows how and precisely when and where to attack God's sons and daughters. Let us first examine the "when" and then delve more deeply into Augustine's understanding of sin to understand the "how."

When? Satan saw how he needed to tempt Adam and Eve before the human family was able to propagate, grow, and thus branch off into various people and lands. Satan knew that if he were in fact going to spoil the *entire* human race, he would have to corrupt the protoparents of all humans thereafter. Think of an infiltrator from Chevrolet who wanted to destroy all the Ford automobiles of a certain model in any given production year. He would be foolish to wait until every one of these Ford cars had come off the assembly line. This malefactor would then have to travel the entire country in an attempt to find where each one of these Fords had been shipped, and then would have to make his way onto every sales lot and destroy each one by hand. The cagiest thing to do would be for the Chevy spy to break into the main Ford plant and sabotage the blueprints before any other production had taken place. Consequently, each and every Ford of that make and model that rolled off the plant would have whatever defect the enemy from Chevrolet had inflicted upon the pattern and prototype. Satan's primal attack worked in the same way: instead of waiting for the human race to increase, he struck at the origin and source of all subsequent human nature. Here he vitiated the human condition at its root, and henceforth all who came forth would be wounded by the pride that wounded Satan in the first place.

How? In his angelic intellect, Satan also knew that there was only one thing for which Adam and Eve had been created of which they did not yet partake. Satan's attempt to malign humanity would never have been effective if he would have tried to tempt us with any natural good. Better company, a more verdant garden, or sweeter foods could not have been held out as enticements. Adam and Eve were planted in Eden for a purpose: to provide them with all the natural goodness they could ever desire. Yet they had never been created for a merely natural purpose, and this is precisely what the enemy will exploit. Satan of course knew this, and he understood that the one thing Adam and Eve did not yet possess was the divinity for which they were brought into being. And so Satan flatteringly said to Eve: "You certainly will not die! God knows well that when you eat of it your eyes will be opened and you will be like gods, who know good and evil" (Gen 3:4–5). One cannot be tempted by something which the tempted has absolutely no idea of or hunger for; and, second, one cannot be tempted by something he or she already possesses. Made in the image and likeness of God, Adam and Eve instinctually knew for whom they were created; made just a free choice away from their final beatitude, Adam and Eve were created to choose godliness, and this is of course precisely what Satan preyed upon.

This is the promise we have been highlighting, the promise God made to us in the Garden of Eden—made in his own divine image and likeness. It is the one promise, therefore, with which the devil could use to tempt us, and Augustine is the first Christian writer to see this move: deification was the only pledge the enemy could have used to tempt those made in and for perfection. On the natural level our first parents had everything supremely and inexhaustibly; on the supernatural level, however, Adam and Eve still lacked the highest and definitive goal for which they had been brought into being—to be like God. This therefore was the *sole enticement* available to Satan—"and you will be like gods" (Gen 3:5).

Augustine translates the seizing of this diabolical offer as the perverse love of one's own power and only then the eventual grasping at one's own omnipotence. It is seeking to be a possessor of divinity and not a partaker, located in the secret curiosity of what life apart from God might be. In this way, the first sin of humankind was not something apparently manifest, for it was done in secret (*in occulto*). For Adam's willful intent to experience life apart from the lavishness offered by his Creator preceded his external act of disobedience. Before Adam and Eve willfully violated the only prohibition they had ever faced, the cunning of Satan already enticed their hearts to toy with the idea that perhaps they could excel and be exalted without any outside interference:

> The devil, therefore, would not have ensnared man in the open and obvious sin of doing what God had forbidden if man had not already begun to be pleased with himself. For it is precisely because he had begun to be pleased with himself that he was also delighted to hear You shall be like gods (Gen 3:5). But they would have been better able to be like gods if they had clung to the true and supreme principle in obedience, instead of taking themselves as their own principle in pride. For created gods are not gods by virtue of any truth of their own

but by virtue of participation in the true God. By grasping for more, then, a person becomes less when, in choosing to be self-sufficient, he defects from the only one who is truly sufficient for him.[29]

Sin for Augustine occurs when I seek to fulfill my divinely intended godliness by my own power—to become God without God. Every sin is thus a shadowy imitation, however futile, to become a sovereign unto oneself, a ripple of the enemy's first blandishment, "you will be like god."

As early as *On True Religion* (390), he saw the meta-motivation of sin to be that of claiming reality for oneself:

> What else, after all, is man seeking in all this but to be the one and only, if that were possible, to whom all things are subject, in perverse imitation, that is to say (*peruersa scilicet imitatio*), of almighty God? And to think that he would have submissively to imitate God by living according to his commandments, and he would have all other things made subject to him and would not sink to such baseness as to be afraid of that beastie who wants to have humanity at his beck and call! So then, pride too has a kind of appetite for unity and omnipotence ... (*Habet ergo et superbia quemdam appetitum unitatis et omnipotentiae*).[30]

This explanation would stay constant throughout his life as a bishop and theologian: in sin, creatures ultimately seek a supremacy, which he understands to be the desire to be like God gone awry. By definition, there can be only one Absolute. Satan attempted to become his own sovereign by turning away from God and now Satan parlays his own wretchedness into ours, seeking to have minions desirous of the same autonomy and shadowy omnipotence Satan himself sought in his refusal to acknowledge God as his sole Lord.

Do we not all do this? It is surely not as galactic or as epic as Lucifer's fall, but very subtly each of us sets ourselves up as the Almighty. How many of us while driving have been aggressively passed or cut off, and we think: "That fool! His driving is so unsafe!"? Yet when I drive that very same speed or

---

[29] *ciu. Dei* 14.13; Babcock, *City of God* (I/7) 120.

[30] *uera rel.* 45.84; Hill, *On True Religion*, as in *On Christian Belief* (I/8) 87; CCL 32.243. See also a few sections later where Augustine defines pride as "a shadowy mimic of genuine freedom and genuine authority," *uera. rel.* 48.93; see also, *en. Ps.* 103, *exp.* 2.11 as well as *ciu. Dei* 12.22 for this desire for self-deification examined under various but similar images.

make that very same maneuver, I think: "It's alright, I'm a good driver," or, "I cannot be late for this appointment," or, "It's okay. I'm in control." How many of us have been in a small setting, a waiting room, in a train car or on an airplane, annoyed by someone on his or her cell phone prattling aimlessly—and loudly? But I find that when I myself take that call, it is because I have a more than good reason, and I am sure "it will be real quick … and, quiet!" Just last week while standing in the security line in an airport, a harried businessman cut right in front of me. My unrehearsed thought was instantly: "What a doofus!" Yet when I have done the very same thing, I justify it by explaining, "Sorry, my plane is in ten minutes …" or, "I just have a quick question …," and so on. Surely we have all caught ourselves condemning others for an action we ourselves can very easily rationalize when it is "I" who am doing it. This is the essence of sin for Augustine: our own self-idolization and twisting of reality that places me above all others, justifying my own actions, and placing myself at the center of what I consider to be real.

The irony is that Augustine knew that we were in fact made to become like God, created to receive and appropriate the divine life so as to enjoy a superhuman existence: eternal, joyful, perfectly loving and wise. But to realize this exalted state, humanity must surrender to God and seek his life on his terms and not on our own. Augustine therefore often uses the scriptural question, "O God, who is your equal?" (Ps 71:19), to preach against the human propensity to rival heaven. To become like God can be done rightly—through proper worship and way of life—or it can be attempted wrongly—through one's own power. Commenting on the psalmist's wonder who is like God here, Augustine begins by asking incredulously,

> Human beings like God? *O God, who is like you?* Nothing … But as for me, says wretched Adam—and Adam is every one of us—look what became of me when I perversely tried to be like you! I am reduced to crying out to you from my captivity … And how did I fall away from you? By seeking in a perverted way to be like you.[31]

We fall back into ourselves when we seek divinity wrongly. The perversion Augustine sees in our futile attempts at self-deification is to become like God apart from God, to become our truest selves by ourselves. It is good and right that we desire to be like God. Are followers of Jesus not told to "be perfect, just as their heavenly Father is perfect" (Mt 5:48)?—but in the fear

---

[31] *en. Ps.* 70, *exp.* 2.6; Boulding, *Expositions* (III/17) 442–3.

of entrusting ourselves to another, we find fault with God's way of fulfilling this promise. For God has arranged our perfection through our humble receptivity, and through our entering into a relationship of love with him and with our neighbor. So we instead resort into our own selves, turn within, and thereby set ourselves up as our own self-centered and localized deities.

In an amazing insight, the former Archbishop of Mexico City, Luis Martinez (1881–1956), wrote that Augustine's dilemma is that he understood well how all human persons were created to become one with God, but in fulfilling that primal vocation wrongly, we cannot help but mix God's love with our own destruction. Archbishop Martinez sees the divided heart as the root of this unfortunate admixture: in our divine imaging, we long to love and to be loved, but in our brokenness, we inevitably lavish sorrow on those we love wrongly:

> Overwhelmed beneath the weight of infinite love, the soul yearns, as St. Augustine did, to be God in order to bestow godlike gifts upon its Beloved. And in its helplessness—cruel and sweet at the same time, as everything is that pertains to love—to compete with sovereign love, the soul endeavors to equalize the infinite riches of God with its own infinitude, with the infinity of misery, and in its audacity, it wishes to supply with sorrow whatever is lacking to its love to make it infinite.[32]

Sensing that we cannot love like Love himself, we turn to sorrow. Refusing the one relationship that will make true love possible, we instead find satisfaction in a lesser reality, our own sadness. This is where we relish the destruction we have made for ourselves, where we long to have company in the misery of our own estrangements.

Augustine knew that this was the sin of pride, and accordingly names such perversion of trying to live apart from the God who creates. This rejection is utterly foolish. Such grasping at autonomy is not only the first sin, it is still the cause of all the sins one can commit. It was a poison which began with Satan, was drunk by Adam and Eve, and still flows through every act of malfeasance today:

> Now pride is a great vice, and the first of vices, the beginning, origin and cause of all sins. It's what cast down an angel and made him into

---

[32]Luis M. Martinez, *Worshipping a Hidden God: Unlocking the Secrets of the Interior Life* (Manchester, NH: Sophia Institute Press [1949] 2014) 77.

the devil. Pride was the cup, which on being cast down he gave the man, still standing up, to drink. He hoisted up into pride one who had been created to the image of God; already unworthy to be so, precisely because he was proud. He envied him, and persuaded him to ignore the law of God, and enjoy his very own power. And how did he persuade him? *If you eat*, he said, *you shall be like gods* (Gn 3:15). He had been made a man, he wished to be a god. He grabbed at what he wasn't, lost what he was. Not that he lost human nature, but he lost both present and future bliss. He lost the place he was to be elevated to, deceived by the one who had been cast down from there.[33]

What emerges is a story wherein an omniscient and omnipotent God chooses to create other persons like himself who can freely love and be loved. But because these creatures are not God, they are brought about *ex nihil*. As such, their lives teeter between the fullness of goodness, God, and the emptiness of nothingness, God's only contrary. Graced with the gift of free will, such creatures are able to choose God or nothing. In choosing nothingness as sin inevitably does, we divine images lose the beautiful human nature God intended for us to have and we "slither and slide down into less and less which is imagined to be more and more, finding satisfaction neither in ourselves nor in anything else as we get further away from him who alone can satisfy us."[34]

This is Augustine's earliest definition of sin and pride, the rational creature's choosing lesser over higher goods. In stressing how all creatures are essentially good, the former Manichee had to define evil not as an existent apart from created goods but, rather, the misguided choosing of lower creatures when opposed to obtainable, higher goods—"for these good things truly are beautiful and lovely in their own way, even though base and mean in comparison with the higher goods that bring us true happiness."[35] In this Christian world, then, no one is able to choose evil directly, but always under the aspect of goodness which every creature maintains to some degree.

A shift in thought is noticeable after 400 AD. Augustine's later thought will recast this earlier sense of pride (as placing creatures over Creator) in terms of the creature's attempt to make private what should otherwise be regarded as

---

[33]*s.* 340A; Hill, *Sermons* (III/9) 295–6.
[34]*Trin.* 10.5.7; Hill, *The Trinity* (I/5) 292; slightly adjusted.
[35]*conf.* 2.5.11; Boulding, *Confessions* (I/1) 69.

common. Sin, again, is an attempt at self-deification but now he explains the establishing of a false creator as the partial's seeking to replace the whole, the private taking precedent over the universal. This etiology of sin estimates how the creature tries to be more than is ontologically possible. Now, one strains to become his or her own god not by participation but by possession, finding delight not by loving all things in God but by sequestering them for oneself:

> What happens is that the soul, loving its own power, slides away from the whole which is common to all into the part which is its own private property. By following God's directions and being perfectly governed by his laws it could enjoy the whole universe of creation; but by the apostasy of pride which is called the beginning of sin it strives to grab something more than the whole and to govern it by its own laws; and because there is nothing more than the whole it is thrust back into anxiety over a part, and so by being greedy for more it gets less ... And so it finds delight in bodily shapes and movements, and because it has not got them with it inside, it wraps itself in their images which it has first fixed in the memory. In this way it defiles itself foully with a fanciful sort of fornication ....[36]

Such a soul pits itself not in God but against him. It finds delight only in that which it can control and place within itself, apart from the demands of community. Or as Augustine warned the Carthaginian catechumen, Honoratus, in 411 or 412, the baptized must seek not their own interests, but the things of Christ: "not pursuing private advantages (*priuata commoda*), but looking out for what is common, in which is found the well-being of all."[37]

The eminent Augustine scholar, Robert Markus, argues that as Augustine seasoned as a pastor, he came to understand pride more communally. Markus maintains that, after the year 400, the Bishop of Hippo focused on pride more as a sin against the social well being of all God's creatures, realized as a selfish individual's internalizing and constructing his or her own reality:

---

[36] *Trin.*, 12.3.14; Hill, *The Trinity* (I/5) 330; see also *ep*. 118.15: on this choosing the private over the universal as the first sin.
[37] *ep*. 140.26.63; Teske, *Letters* (II/2) 276.

Augustine's thought in his fifties began to be dominated by the notion that the roots of sin lie in the self's retreat into a privacy which is deprivation: the self is deprived of community. All community—with God, with one's fellows, and even with one's own self—is fatally ruptured by sin. The radical flaw in human nature is now transcribed in terms of a retreat into a closed-off self.[38]

This "retreat into a closed-off self" signifies a more mature understanding of that innate desire to be like God, now seen as the dismissal of true reality and the running away into my own self at the cost of communion and other-centered intimacy. This is the something the fallen *imago Dei* is tempted to do when our memories, intellects, and wills are not in union with the transcendent God. In Book 12 of *De Trinitate*, we hear how the fallen soul falls in love with itself wrongly by seizing a partial but private property (*priuatem partem*). In this, the soul shows how enamored with its own power it can become, and, as Augustine will both celebrate and lament, the created soul is that one creature which can see itself to be comparable to God himself (*Videtur mihi esse similis Deo*).[39]

The soul's likeness to God is of course its greatest dignity but in its fallenness it seeks to displace God. This is the apostasy of pride, manifested as the soul's delight in itself (or in a mere creature), seeking to sequester reality for itself:

> ... when it is happy, the soul itself is not happy because of its own good; otherwise it would never be unhappy ... For when the soul rejoices in itself, because of itself, as if then because of its own good, it is proud ... Ceasing in that way and subsiding from its own boasting and inflatedness, it strives to cling to God (*inhaerere Deo*) and to be re-created and reformed ... The first sin, that is, the first voluntary defect, is to rejoice over one's power.[40]

This is the sad paradox of sin: we could have become like God fully and without reservation if we would have only let God fulfill our image and likeness as he desired and not as we determined. We were put in Eden

---

[38]Robert Markus, *Conversion and Disenchantment in Augustine's Spiritual Career* (Villanova, PA: Villanova University Press, 1989) 31–2.
[39]*quant.* 2.3; CSEL 89.133.
[40]*ep.* 118.15; Teske, *Letters* (II/2) 113.

together, "male and female he created them" (Gen 1:27b). This was so we would know *ab initio* that we were made for communion and that the highest goods in this world are always relational, always other-centered. Sin, on the other hand, always proves to be solipsistic, a turning in on oneself in the futile desire of possessing all that is. It is a desire to be whole and perfect autonomously, which is paradigmatic of all sin: "Sin, however, is a disorder and a perversion (*inordinatio atque peruersitas*) in the human being—that is, a turning away from the creator, who is more excellent, and a turning to created things, which are inferior."[41] Augustine well knows that the created will is not able to will well unless God effects in it the desire to collaborate with grace, but he also knows that the created will cannot not love. Not loving is never an option for persons, human, and divine. The question is: What will one love? If one loves what is properly loveable, a good love arises; if one loves wrongly, an evil love: "*recta itaque uoluntas est bonus amor et uoluntas peruersa malus amor.*"[42] The soul inevitably and ineluctably seeks wholeness. It longs to love and to be loved. The struggle comes when we convince ourselves we can do this alone and on our own terms. However, all human flourishing for Augustine will inevitably prove relational; all stagnation and sin, on the other hand, solipsistic.

Conclusion

This chapter has hopefully helped us see that the reality of sin for Augustine is contingent upon wills that are created so as to be able to choose freely. When turned toward God, that free will results in freedom; when turned in on itself, that free will is one day realized as imprisonment. As far as Augustine can tell, even that latter choice to pursue oneself, to pursue the world, is undertaken for the sake of some good. There are no evil things for this former Manichean, only the evil use of good things. That is why sin is defined as the moment one chooses to turn away from the ultimate Good and chooses another quite lower:

> ... with his freedom of choice he chose to turn aside to lower things and forsake the higher, to lend his ears to the serpent and close his ears to God, and set fairly and squarely between instructor and seducer,

---

[41] *Simpl.* 1.2.18; Teske, *Responses to Miscellaneous Questions* (I/12) 200.
[42] *ciu. Dei* 14.7; CCL 47.422.

to comply rather with the seducer than with the instructor. He heard the devil, after all, with exactly the same ears as he heard God. So why didn't he rather trust the better of the two?[43]

Augustine goes on to answer that Adam chose not to listen to God because he instead decided to trust in his own well being than to think he needed help when still unaffected by disease. But God is a physician always and our life depends on staying in union with him: some (like Adam and Eve) need his services in order not to fall into disease, the rest of us need him to have our health restored. Either way, the self-indulgence of Adam led him to trust a creature that he could easily behold, immediately understand (so he thought) and was beguiled into his misdirected imitation and seizing of divinity.

With Gen 3:5 echoing through every misuse of free will, Augustine is thus able to descry in every sin an attempt to be one's own sovereign, an establishing of an alien god. This is a god not characterized by personal relationship, the perfect triune other-centeredness as Augustine the Catholic would later come to understand. No, this is a monadic and absorptive deity who commands the dissolution of otherness. To be god is to ensure no one else is: my world, my power, my status. The radical temptation toward sin, then, is to become a deity not like the Father, Son, and Holy Spirit whom Augustine will come to wholeheartedly worship, but a pagan god with no intrinsic and inextricable identification with truth and self-giving love.

When one commits oneself to such a position, the self and the world in which one finds oneself is marked only by hostility and warring factions. There is only division and alienation, as well as the consequent fear of intimacy and communion. I must protect myself; I must surrender to no one. Would union with another be obliterative? But as Augustine will come to see, those who have been brought into existence by another should know that their progenitor could not order anything injurious toward them. The true Creator of life does not bring others about their excellence. Once he left the divided cosmos of the Manicheans, this is how Augustine came to view Eden: the man has been established to live trusting the Lord and knowing in his ways his own excellence. Acting almost as a foreshadowing of the pear tree scene taken up in the next chapter, it is not the fruit of the tree that is at stake, it is the relationship and the reliance that such fruit symbolizes. Let us now turn to treat the famous scene of the theft of pears as recorded in the second book of Augustine's *Confessions*.

---

[43] *s.* 278.2; Hill, *Sermons* (III/8) 51.

CHAPTER 3
THOSE PEARS: SIN AS SELF-SABOTAGE

I had one sweet hour of repose when all my jobs were finished and divided it between another instalment of Marcel Proust—*Le côte de Guermantes*—and the *Confessions of St. Augustine* ... of the two I would rather read St. Augustine. It is like a painting by Morland set over an altar. Rum thing to see a man making a mountain out of robbing a pear tree in his teens.

— Oliver Wendell Holmes to Harold Laski[1]

Late in his life the United States Supreme Court Justice, Oliver Wendell Holmes (d. 1935), sat Augustine squarely in the dock and scrutinized his *Confessions*, posing a question most readers throughout the centuries have asked as well: Why does Augustine recall the stealing of that infamous fruit so many years later? Of all the stupid stunts, is this really the worst thing he did as a boy? Perhaps he has become nothing more than a scrupulous adult. Surely of all the evil exploits which could have surfaced as he looked back on his life, why would the contrite Bishop of Hippo select this relatively innocuous and random pilfering of pears? Justice Holmes suggests that time with the *Confessions* is like time before an oil by the London-born painter George Morland (1763–1804). Like Morland's stills, Augustine too decorates the story of his life with day-to-day scenes which at first glance seem particularly common and unimportant, fairly "rum" as Holmes quips, but in time actually show forth an allure drawing the reader into the most essential aspects of the human condition.

This chapter revolves around the key parts of the picture Augustine paints in this scene of his *Confessions*, a work which still stands as one of the most unique and unmatched pieces of theological literature to date.

---

[1] Oliver Wendell Holmes, *Holmes-Laski Letters: The Correspondence of Mr. Justice Holmes and Harold J. Laski, 1916–35*, ed., Mark DeWolfe Howe (Cambridge, MA: Harvard University Press, 1953) 300. Fredrich Nietzsche also took a mocking tone when discussing Augustine's guilt over the pears in a letter to a friend (dated March 31,1885): "Oh this old rhetor! How false he is and how distorted his vision! How I laughed (e.g., about the 'theft' of his youth, basically a student story)"; Briefwechsel: Kritische Gesamtausgabe, vol. 3 (Berlin, 1982) 3.34 as in Robin Lane Fox, *Augustine: Conversions in Confessions* (New York: Basic Books, 2015) 66.

Composed just prior to the year 400, Augustine needed to prove to the North African world that he had returned from Italy contrite and converted for all the things for which he had long been known–a former new-ager with the Manichean sect, a sexually exploitative youth who admittedly sought countless libidinal escapades, and one who landed the top oratory post in the empire through the backroom politicking of the leading pagan of the day, Quintus Aurelius Symmachus. But as we all knew before we picked this story up, God's providence would prove greater than Augustine's malfeasance. Through all the circuitous wanderings of Augustine's life, the gentle Lord would come to bring about sanctity from his sin and holiness from his hollowness.

We have seen so far that the Triune God created other persons so as to enjoy eternal communion through their free conversion toward him. This metanoia can be neither simultaneously automatic nor impersonally forced, but God's creative act includes this invitation for creatures endowed with their own free will to choose God over the innate ability to put oneself before one's Creator (Chapter 1). The devil, however, refused to acknowledge anyone else at the center of his world and in his pride Satan turned away, choosing self over God and becoming content with a self-imposed alienation: "Which way I fly is hell; myself am hell."[2] Satan grew comfortable with the uncomfortable, too familiar with the hell he has become. In this frustrated desire to be his own deity, he seeks to bring others to him. Augustine knew how sin never turns in on just itself but inevitably affects others, and part of this diabolical pride is to impede human persons' communion with God. So, from examining the angelic fall from grace, we traversed downward to Eden and the sin of Adam and Eve (Chapter 2). While essentially different types of created persons, sinful angels and sinful humanity both share the same fallen desire to be gods without God.

In imitating the angelic insurgence in putting themselves in place of the truly divine, Adam and Eve also acted as if they could find fulfillment and wholeness without the Author of all they desired. We all teeter between the God who created us and the "nothingness" from which he brought us. With these themes now highlighted, we are ready to turn to one of the most iconic moments in Augustine's life, his stealing of the pears in *conf.* 2. In the words of the University of Notre Dame's John Cavadini, this boyhood thievery was no mere teenage shenanigan, but in fact is meant to stand

---

[2]Milton, *Paradise Lost*, 4.75.

as Augustine's "metaphysical window into the problem of evil."[3] So, why did Augustine steal that which he neither wanted nor needed? Why did he transgress what he knew to be proper conduct for no other reason than his own destruction?

We shall answer this murky question into the choosing of evil by first examining the pear tree scene as it appears in *conf.* 2. This memorable event is confessed not only as an ethical failure to be forgiven, but also as an opportunity to raise more profound existential questions. As he admits at the outset of the second book: "Now I want to call to mind the foul deeds I committed, those sins of the flesh that corrupted my soul, not in order to love them, but to love you, my God."[4] After we move through the key images intended by Augustine, we move on to the second and larger question. Five aspects of this scene will be lifted from Augustine's hands to be assessed and understood more deeply.

The second section of this chapter thus hopes to answer why we act against our own good, even when there is no good to be gained. In other words, what account could Augustine (and any of us) give for relishing our own ruin and seemingly enjoying that ease in falling into decay? What we hope to uncover is the sad irony of our postlapsarian souls. There is something within each of us that simply doesn't like some part of ourselves, something deep within the lovesick heart that finds some sort of twisted comfort embracing one's own ruin. It is the cutter whose scars bring comfort to her in the slicing reminder that life still flows under the surface. It is the addict who assures himself that the numbing familiarity he seeks is—surely this time—just one more fix, one last violent outburst, or one final pornographic image away. While today's diagnostic manuals scramble to stay current with such behavior, Augustine captured a facet of this phenomenon over a millennium and a half ago—someone who was never content to remain a relic of the past, but instead sought to confess in a style that muted the particulars so as to magnify the perennial. In this way he invites each of us to hear not only his own life's story, but the story of Adam, the story of Christ, and the story of every person hungry for wholeness.

---

[3]John Cavadini, "Book Two: Augustine's Book of Shadows," *A Reader's Guide to Augustine's Confessions*, ed., Kim Paffenroth and Robert P. Kennedy (Louisville, Westminster John Knox Press, 2003) 25–34; 29.

[4]*conf.* 2.1.1.; Boulding, *Confessions* (I/1) 62.

Dynamics of the pear tree scene: *Confessions* 2.4.9-.10.18

Augustine's most celebrated and enduring work is certainly his ground-breaking *Confessions*. Hippo Regius, a relatively insignificant seaside port, now finds itself with two bishops. Not only old and weakening, the current bishop Valerius is admittedly not from Augustine's North Africa and apparently not fluent in Punic nor overly competent in Latin, unable to keep the Catholics strong and the Donatists at bay.[5] Bishop Valerius has therefore requested permission for a younger upstart like Augustine to help him preach and shepherd his flock. It is this new call to be a large public figure in Christ's Church that sets Augustine to take up his ink, to let the wider world know that as real as his waywardness was, his Christian conversion has been even more formative. So, in or around the year 397, Augustine sets to work to vindicate Valerius's decision to ask the Carthaginian Metropolitan Megalius for a coadjutor bishop (in accord with the canons of the Council of Nicaea) which, although not totally unheard of at this time, was not yet a common practice.

Known to many in North Africa as a former Manichean, a pagan sympathizer, and somewhat of a ne'er do well, Augustine humbly yet unabashedly reviews his past to bring to light the many ways he sinned against Christ and his Church: Nine years in a bizarre cult, his fascination with astrology, and his sexual failures for which he felt particularly guilty. But of all these offenses against Christ, one thing stands out as the epitome of his past. Of all the sins this middle-aged man could have retrieved, it is the seemingly harmless stealing of some fruit that symbolizes for him the deprivations of the human heart. William Mann looks and sees "one of the most philosophically perplexing passages" in all of Augustine's writings.[6] Scott MacDonald calls it "Augustine's most extreme piece of self-flagellation. He appears to scourge himself mercilessly for what might best be described as a bit of late-night adolescent mischief."[7] So, what is going on? Why this disconnect between the deep power of sin and the mischiefs of some callow youth so many years prior? What is Augustine telling us by recalling this scene so vividly at length, filling up most of the second book of his stylistically well-thought-out *Confessions*?

---

[5]This is admitted in the *Unfinished Commentary on Romans* [*ep. Rm. inch.*] §13.
[6]William E. Mann, *God, Belief, and Perplexity* (Oxford: Oxford University Press, 2016) 27.
[7]Scott MacDonald, "Petit Larceny, the Beginning of All Sin: Augustine's Theft of the Pears," *Augustine's Confessions: Critical Essays*, ed., William E. Mann (Lanham, MD: Rowman & Littlefield, 2006) 46.

The answer I set forth here is that this particular evening is still burning in Augustine's memory not because of the matter of the theft but because of its motive. As we shall see, he engaged in this communal act of theft not because of any real reason—he had better fruit at home, he wasn't hungry, and so on—but simply because he loved tasting his own destruction. He commits a crime not out of the normal reasons of personal conquest, financial gain, long-awaited revenge, sexual satisfaction, or a myriad other reasons any of us know all too well. Here Augustine steals not out of inordinate love of some perceived good, but out of a twisted fascination with evil, and such dissolution raises a very important question in his mind that he is still wrestling with decades later. Reading Augustine's own retrospective on this infamous evening still sends shivers down one's spine: not in need of any fruit, actually possessing better fruit at home, he commits the sinful act of theft simply because he ravished the feel of his own ruin.

Looking back over the whole of his life, Augustine chooses this scene from his sixteenth year to show posterity the powerful allure of decay. If this were just the rascally ruse of some bored youths, a carousing evening costing some local farmers a few measly pieces of produce, our author surely would not have given it another moment's thought; but it is still raw in Augustine's memory many decades later. Why so? To answer this, let us now quote at length the salient sentences of this scene.

> Beyond question, theft is punished by your law, O Lord (Ex 20:15; Dt 5:19), and by the law written in human hearts (Rom 2:14–15), which not even sin itself can erase; for does any thief tolerate being robbed by another thief, even if he is rich and the other is driven by want? I was under no compulsion of need, unless a lack of moral sense can count as need, and a loathing for justice, and a greedy, full-fed love of sin. Yet I wanted to steal, and steal I did. I already had plenty of what I stole, and of much better quality too, and I had no desire to enjoy it when I resolved to steal it. I simply wanted to enjoy the theft for its own sake, and the sin.
>
> Close to our vineyard there was a pear tree laden with fruit. This fruit was not enticing, either in appearance or in flavor. We nasty lads went there to shake down the fruit and carry it off at dead of night, after prolonging our games out of doors until that late hour according to our abominable custom. We took enormous quantities, not to feast on ourselves but perhaps to throw to the pigs; we did eat a few, but that was not our motive: we derived pleasure from the deed simply because it was forbidden.

Look upon my heart, O God, look upon this heart of mine, on which you took pity in its abysmal depths. Enable my heart to tell you now what it was seeking in this action which made me bad for no reason, in which there was no motive for my malice except malice. The malice was loathsome, and I loved it. I was in love with my own ruin, in love with decay: not with the thing for which I was falling into decay but with decay itself, for I was depraved in soul, and I leapt down from your strong support into destruction, hungering not for some advantage to be gained by the foul deed, but for the foulness of it.[8]

Along with the conversion scene of Augustine (*conf.* 8.12.29) and the communal ascent with Monica in Ostia (*conf.* 9.10.23-.13.37), this is the most celebrated moment in Augustine's spiritual journey. It is the longest dissection of a particular sin in any of the *Confessions*. The disobedience, the conversion, the mystical experience—all happen within the context of a garden setting, they each involve his free embracing of some new reality, and all become watershed moments in this pilgrim's story.

Book 2 of the *Confessions* opened with Augustine's asking God to heal this self-imposed alienation. He begs God to recollect him into a unified self, praying for the grace—"to give a coherent account of my disintegrated self, for when I turned away from you, the one God, and pursued a multitude of things, I went to pieces."[9] Telling his story to the God who really emerges as the main actor throughout the *Confessions*, Augustine seeks to be unified, to be regathered into an integrated and wholly purposeful self. Conversely, recalling the pear tree event is to occasion Augustine's thinking on the metanarrative of disintegration itself. As modern-day jargon puts it, he has to "name, claim, and tame" this gnawing feeling so many years later, having acted wrongly for really no reason. In this way it was a maliciousness capturing all other malice, the very essence of self-imposed destruction and annihilation. As he sees it, this is the human attempt to become one's own deity, to become a god over all else. That is why after this "narrative window" of the pear tree, he admits: "All those who wander far away and set themselves up against you are imitating you, but in a perverse way …

---

[8]*conf.* 2.4.9; Boulding, *Confessions* (I/1) 67–8.

[9]*conf.* 2.1.1; Boulding, *Confessions* (I/1) 62; James O'Donnell, "The Coincidence Points to a Late Antique Habit of Thought That Perceived the World-as-Experienced as a Place of Shards and Fragments, and Supplemented That Perception with a Yearning for Wholeness," *Augustine: Confessions*, vol. II: *Commentary on Books 1–7* (Oxford: Clarendon Press, 1992) 21–2, commenting on *conf.* 1.3.3.

trying to simulate a crippled sort of freedom, attempting a shady parody of omnipotence."[10] As we outlined previously in Chapter 2, instead of seeking to rely on the one, true God, the sinner attempts to become one's own god. In this waywardness, the sinner flees from the Trinity of communion and cohesion, preferring to set him or herself up as a deity wobbling upon one's own distortion of divinity. Deep down we may know that we are *not* God, but at least at this moment of maliciousness, I am in control, able to do what I want as I want with no real demands upon me.

When he was only sixteen years old, Augustine commits what most of us today would consider a seemingly harmless act, the stealing of some pears. Yet this still bothers him so rawly as an adult, he includes it as the centerpiece of the second chapter of his life's history. To understand why this still gnaws at our author, we have to commit ourselves to how he sees reality—as that which teeters between the fullness of all being, God, and the nothingness from which God created all things. That is, for Augustine, every created existent carries traces of both God and nothing; for created persons gifted with free will, then, the ability to choose the fullness of reality or the utter emptiness of nothing is a constant possibility. In the words of Carol Harrison, the free human agent turns either "towards God or turns away from him into nothingness."[11] Is this why the pear theft plays such a central role in his recalling of these sacred memories? Is this what is closest in Augustine's mind to the possibility of choosing nothing? He seeks nothing beyond the evil he entertains—he wants neither the fruit nor the sordid company that is achieved by such carousing. Here there is no satisfaction described, no contentment realized; there is no savoring of the fresh fruit just plucked, and no booty to be enjoyed later. Augustine simply enjoys the feeling of ruin and self-destruction, and this is a quandary he never quite fully understood.

Before we take up this paradox of loving one's own destruction, let us first highlight five noteworthy flourishes of this scene. The first is the fact that it is set in a garden with distant echoes from that first place of divine disobedience, the Garden of Eden. The second observation Augustine wants us to note is the fact that this theft was done under the guise of darkness. The third lesson comes as we hear the Parable of the Prodigal Son reverberate throughout Augustine's own account. The fourth is found in Augustine's description of his fall from grace, an intentional leap down

---

[10]*conf.* 2.6.14; Boulding, *Confessions* (I/1) 71.
[11]Carol Harrison, "Augustine and Religious Experience," *Louvain Studies* 27 (2002) 99–118; 105.

from the Father. The fifth is found in Augustine's philosophy of community. The "herd mentality" seems to be the closest thing our author can provide as a coherent answer to why he stole what was not his, what was not even all that pleasant or useful.

After we examine these five important aspects of Augustine's youthful crime, we are in a good place to examine this pear tree scene by showing why Augustine thinks this theft is essentially different than other crimes— there was absolutely nothing to be gained. Here the great paradox of this act comes into view: unlike other wrongdoings, Augustine neither needed nor even enjoyed the pears. In a raw and unguarded reflection, he admits that he did this only because he was in love with his own ruin, desirous to destroy himself.

(1) The significance of the tree

As we saw in the previous chapter, Adam and Eve come to be in a Garden and stand before a God-given tree, a good creature, and are offered a choice, the choice: God or self? In the Garden of Calvary, Augustine's Savior hung on a tree to atone for this disobedience and for all acts of maliciousness from Eden onward. Three days later, as one mistaken for a gardener (Jn 20:15), this same Jesus has defeated sin and has risen to new life. Augustine appreciated Ponticianus's account of how the two court officials at Trier came to embrace Christian holiness while walking in a garden,[12] he humbly realized God's call for him to enter his Church while meditating one providential day in a garden,[13] and he and his mother spend their last hours together gazing out over an Ostian *hortus intra domum*—a garden within the house.[14]

Moreover, the Manichean mythology which Augustine had not that long ago abandoned as he composed his *Confessions*, held an important place for the role of trees—those bearers of divinity who wept when plucked and whose "mother tree too wept milky tears."[15] In the words of Carl Vaught,

---

[12]*conf.* 8.6.15. For a survey of the importance of trees and wood in the works of Augustine, see Leo Ferrari, "The Tree in the Works of Saint Augustine," *Augustiniana* 38:1 (1988) 37–53.

[13]*conf.* 8.8.19-.12.30; note too how Augustine in his preconversion struggle likens himself to the Adam, the first man in a garden (*conf.* 8.10.23).

[14]*conf.* 9.10.23; now that Augustine is presenting himself for official entry into the Catholic Church, he extols his mother, both biological and ecclesial, and now situates the garden (*hortus*) within this new eternal home (*domus*).

[15]*conf.* 3.10.18; Boulding, *Confessions* (I/1) 88.

Manicheans believe that trees spring from the semen of demons and are a rich source of particles that have escaped the Kingdom of Light. A Manichean would never pluck their fruit and even if he did so accidentally, he would ask of the Manichean elect to ingest it to release the light. From a Manichean perspective, giving the fruit to an animal ("we did throw some to the pigs") would increase the disgrace of the crime, embedding the goodness of the particles in it in creatures lower in the chain of being than trees.[16]

Augustine was one of those *auditores* who were instructed to bring such fruit to a member of the elect, so that "when he belched or groaned in prayer he would spew out angels, or even particles of God."[17] Did he then recall this furtive night in the orchard with a bit of delight, some Schadenfreude, knowing how recalling this moment of throwing loads of fruit imbued with Manichean divinity would bring only frustration and cries of condemnation from his former cult?

There is still much more than an anti-Manichean trope however. In situating his first real moral struggle in a garden before a tree which will determine Augustine's destiny, *conf.* 2.4.9-.10.18 is meant to bring the reader back to that primal and ultimate place of decision. To whom shall one be faithful? Do I live in a "garden" of my own toil and securing, or do I enjoy the life I have as a gift with the gift-giver ever present? This is what Adam decided for all and what Christ has come to remedy: both did it on a tree, both had to wrestle in a garden.

Augustine made sure that his readers understood there are diverse ways to understand the Garden in Genesis. While some commentators take it as only a material description (*corporaliter*), our author wants to elevate our reading and insist that Eden also stands metaphorically for many spiritual blessings and perfections. Augustine never disagrees that Eden is not some real place, verdant and plush, but he also needs to show there is more than just "a most delightful place."[18] There is an allegorical significance to the garden built into his literal reading: it is a place of divine decision, a place real and wooded surrounded with all natural perfections, but also a place

---

[16]Carl G. Vaught, *The Journey toward God in Augustine's Confessions, Books I–VI* (Albany: SUNY Press, 2003) 55.

[17]*conf.* 3.10.18; Boulding, *Confessions* (I/1) 89.

[18]*Gn. litt.* 8.1.4; Hill, *Genesis* (I/13) 349.

where malevolence can lurk, slithering slowly into a space that has opened itself up to the parasitical possibilities of evil.

Yet the garden need not have had distorted so. Augustine notices that the unfallen human race has two commands to keep. After the first command to be fertile and multiply (Gen 1:28), which was natural and understandable enough, the second is not to eat of the Tree of the Knowledge of Good and Evil (Gen 2:16–17). Compared to that natural need for Adam and Eve to raise up new offspring, this second commandment proves more mysterious, more in need of trust. For this command was not meant simply to continue natural life, but to begin to teach the human race of its supernatural destiny. For having been made for God, in his image and likeness, the human person ultimately finds his or her vocation in obeying God's call, insisting on God's ways, and eventually appropriating his divine life by partaking of his very nature (2 Pet 1:4).

Yet, as we stressed in the previous chapter, there must be something inherently noxious about this tree in particular. God's commands are never capricious for Augustine, and so the Tree of the Knowledge of Good and Evil is surely the kind of tree that when one eats of it, such a one is harmed. God's commands warn us, therefore, not to eat of this tree not because God simply says so but this is the kind of tree whose fruit one should never consume. This tree is good; it is clearly and unapologetically part of God's good creation. However, the eating of the fruit is harmful to humans and so God warns against it, it is not God's warning that makes the fruit harmful. As any good creature, the harm to humans comes when this good is used wrongly, when its fruit is consumed by one whose constitution would find it necessarily toxic.

Here in *Confessions* 2 the pear tree is surely to evoke that ancient image, that first tree under a command which would sadly result in disobedience. But that is not the final word, for it was most fitting that the New Adam restore human obedience and thus bring divine union about by means of a tree as well. The cross for Augustine therefore stands as the fulfillment of the Edenic tree. This is a standard patristic parallel, and it appears often in Augustine. For instance, in his *Answer to Julian*,

Hence, Adam is the symbol of Christ. They ask: In what way is he the symbol? As Adam became the cause of death for those who are born from him, though they did not eat from the tree, so Christ has become for those who are born from him, even if they have done nothing righteous, the source of the righteousness which he gave to all of us through the cross.[19]

From a tree our self-alienation originated in Adam, from a tree our salvation arose in Christ, and with Augustine's tree full of pears, that olden battle continues.

But the tree can also be a place of redemption. As the Apostle Paul penetrates Augustine's soul with the admonition which our struggling seeker is finally able to hear: "Not in dissipation and drunkenness, nor in debauchery and lewdness, nor in arguing and jealousy; but put on the Lord Jesus Christ, and make no provision for the flesh or the gratification of your desires" (Rom 13:13–14), Augustine wants to make sure his audience knows he experienced this watershed moment only when he had "flung myself down somehow under a fig tree."[20] Did he really take the time to note the type of tree at such a crucial moment of his spiritual odyssey? Is this fig tree supposed to remind us of the choice made in Eden (Gen 3:7) or the fruitfulness expected when the Lord of all life draws near (Mt 21:19; Mk 11:13–14), or both? Either way, Augustine sees how some very crucial moments of his life, of all life, are determined in the shadows, wrestled with under a tree. Whether it be the disobedience of Adam, the life-giving cross of Christ, or Augustine's own impactful decisions, the pear tree early on in the *Confessions* is much more than a woody plant, representing a myriad of meanings upon which each reader is invited to reflect.

(2) The dead of night

Darkness has been a timeless metaphor for dissolution. The day brings about growth, ripening and maturation. Daytime is when things shine, are purified and made apparent; the nighttime scares and can mask things for what they truly are. Augustine makes sure we know that this theft from the pear tree happened in the night, and that like the first Adam, he had become "like that servant of yours who fled from his Lord and hid in the shadows" as well.[21] Later this insight is translated into a pastoral tone as the Bishop consistently teaches his parishioners, "It's bad to go out into the dark; it's

---

[19]*c. Jul.* 1.27, Teske, *Answer to the Pelagians* II (I/24) 286.
[20]*conf.* 8.12.28; Boulding, *Confessions* (I/1) 206.
[21]*conf.* 2.6.14; Boulding, *Confessions* (I/1) 71.

good to come into the light, where there is absolutely no other darkness at all, neither of the heart nor of the flesh."[22]

The darkness of Gen 1:3 thus became for Augustine an image of the fallen angels and it is the darkness they control still. The darkness that is bemoaned here is not an ontological reality, as all created things are good; it is a moral state which finds the goodness of God so repugnant, it has to be separated (*diuisit*; Augustine notes it is not *creauit*) from the Lord's presence.[23] As we traced in the previous chapter, such an interpretation allows Augustine to account for both the creation of the angels within the Genesis narrative as well as the beginning of the angelic fall. It is the darkness that represents that latter sad new reality, with Satan now known as the father of all darkness (Eph 6:12), and Paul would not name him and his minions "princes of darkness unless they were princes of sinners and lords of the wicked."[24] Unlike his former Manichean commitment, darkness now is not a separate divine substance but the result of divine aversion. The tenebrous angels are not intrinsically evil, however, their turning from the Light casts a shadow not only through their very being forever, but also enables sinners like Augustine to seek out furtive goods that the sun might have never permitted.

This is why the garden, like this entire earthly realm, is a place of light and shadow, a place of decision between heaven and hell. It is not yet the true life but it is the only way there. In a very early sermon (c. 391), Augustine teaches that:

> This life, in fact, should rather be called the shade or shadow of life. Nor is it without significance that Adam the fugitive, after the offense of his sin, hid from the face of the Lord by covering himself with the leaves of trees, which provide dark shady places—*like one fleeing his Lord*, as it says, *and reaching shade*.[25]

The treacherous Judas even becomes darkness itself when he leaves the upper room (*Erat autem nox, et ipse qui exiuit, erat nox*), commencing the betrayal of Jesus on the night of the Last Supper.[26] Virtue illumines; evil beclouds. Accordingly, all sinners live in the shadows, in a world not wholly illusory

---

[22]*s*. 125A.4; Hill, *Sermons* (III/4) 267.
[23]Cf. *ciu. Dei* 11.19–20.
[24]*ep. Jo.* 1.5; Hill, *Homilies on the First Epistle of John* (I/14) 25.
[25]*s*. 351.3; Hill, *Sermons* (III/10) 121.
[26]*Jo. eu. tr.* 62.6; CCL 36.485.

but not yet wholly real either. The shadows must therefore be detected and thus discerned so as to see whether they are helping hide our misdeeds or are goading us on to the true light.

(3) The prodigal wanders

The third important aspect to appear in this narrative is how this snippet of Augustine's sixteenth year is couched in terms of the Parable of the Prodigal Son. Book 2 of the *Confessions* opens with overtures of wandering and seeking sustenance in a land of immediate destruction (*conf.* 2.1.1) and ends with the honest admittance that Augustine has "wandered away, my God; far from your steadfastness I strayed in adolescence, and I became to myself a land of famine."[27] As readers make their way through this book, we are brought to the pear tree scene, and are immediately struck with the gravity Augustine intends to convey. Here is another and perhaps even more destructive Prodigal who has wandered from his father's house in order to carouse and to fritter away his otherwise fruitful birthright. In fact, this rebellion involves a distant place, a misuse of God's good creation, and (eventually) a contrition that will bring our boy back. On top of his casting himself obviously in the role of another prodigal son, the former Manichean is also signaling how he has come to recognize his once held fallacy of the good god's identification with fruit. That which should be honored and ritually consumed, the pears are carelessly thrown to the swine. Such ingratitude mirrors the Prodigal's same wretchedness (cf., Lk 15:11–32), and the thing that would surely cast the Manichean mind into convulsions is to see fruit plucked for no reason and cast onto the ground simply to rot and be consumed by unclean pigs and lower creatures of all sorts. Such sacrilege would be too much, a wickedly clever move on the former Manichean author's part.

All of these components are, not surprising, found in Augustine's homilies on the Parable of the Prodigal Son. Whereas the Jews are represented by the older son who has always had the law but finds mercy hard to come by, the prodigal is the Gentiles who tend to waste their lives on luxury, idols, and depravity of all sorts. To them both the Christ has come. When expounding Luke 15, Augustine calls the incarnate Son the "arm of the Father" who uses the Incarnation to *run out and meet us* (Lk 15:20). Through Jesus's power continued through the Church's sacraments, the sinner is welcomed back

---

[27] *conf.* 2.10.18; Boulding, *Confessions* (I/1) 74.

to his or her true home which makes life light and purposeful, something Augustine in his sixteenth year could have only imagined.[28]

Life is difficult and we run away only when we fail to love properly. Augustine sees in the Prodigal's wandering an aimlessness which is the result of a disordered set of commitments. Loving correctly keeps us close to the Father because we trust him and allow him to tend to our every need. In rebellion, however, the ungrateful children turn their back on what is real and alone fulfilling, and instead search for what will in the end only disappoint:

> Do those who love themselves really have confidence in themselves? They begin by forsaking God to love themselves, and then are driven out of themselves to love what is outside themselves … (then alluding to the Prodigal son) … he first returns to himself in order to return to the one from whom he had fallen, in falling from himself. He had fallen from his father, he had fallen from himself. He had gone away from himself to things outside. He comes back to himself and sets off to his father, where he can keep himself in the utmost security.[29]

This is the youthful Augustine, searching for love only by following the extensions of his own fallen desires. He is away from himself by refusing to go into his truest self, refusing to go back to the Father who can alone offer the embrace of security. Unwilling to rest there, however, all Prodigals find themselves in a land of famine (*regio egestatis*). This is our Augustine in *conf.* 2 where he sadly hungers after his own sinfulness, choosing to traverse ever further from the only source of satisfaction.

This is ultimately a problem of self-love. In leaving the Father, the Prodigal chooses to love himself by himself, a move impossible for Augustine:

> If your works are not praise offered to God, you are beginning to be in love with yourself, and to join the company of those people whom

---

[28]Furthermore, Augustine preaches that the Son goes to the prodigal and by imposing virtue upon him, does not weigh him down but actually lifts him up from the earth (Mt 11:30). There are three things that one can put on one's back: that which will weigh him down much, that which is hardly noticeable it is so light, and that which paradoxically elevates, and this is the way Christ's commandments are: "Observe it in the case or birds. Every bird carries its wings … Do you consider they are burdened by them? Let them remove the burden, and they will fall"; *s.* 112A.6; Hill, *Sermons* (III/4) 157.

[29]*s.* 96.2; Hill, *Sermons* (III/4) 30.

the apostle predicts, *They will be lovers of themselves* (2 Tm 3:2). Find no pleasure in yourself, and let him be your delight who made you; because what you find displeasing in yourself is what you yourself brought about in you ... Give back to him his own gifts; do not try to snatch a share of your inheritance and go off abroad, there to squander it on harlots and feed pigs.[30]

This is the root of all sin, sequestering what is God's and attempting to live a life without him. Sin for Augustine is ingratitude, that fallen tendency to think of all that is gift as all that I have for myself, and this is precisely what Lucifer inaugurated.

(4) Fall from grace

The fourth component of the pear tree scene is found in Augustine's description that in sinning he had in fact "leapt down from [God's] strong support" into his own self-sufficiency. Is this not an echo of Lucifer's own leap (Is 14:12) from the Father's embrace into his own hell? Does Augustine not introduce this book by admitting that his adolescence was a time when he was blazing to be filled with hell? Lucifer is the first cast downward (Ez 28:16–17), as God the Father becomes the first to have ever lost a son. The dissatisfied Augustine presents himself here as an echo of the devil's first fall from heavenly grace. Augustine the Prodigal has similarly reached the periphery of autonomy, above any restriction or commitment and has chosen to dwell apart from his loving Father's embrace. Book 2 of the *Confessions* opens, after all, with Augustine's admittance that as an adolescent he could not wait to be filled with the fires of hell (*inferis*), and even relates this confession to the dynamic of a tree and the shadows that inevitably fall from it:

There was a time in adolescence when I was afire to take my fill of hell. I boldly thrust out rank, luxuriant growth in various furtive love affairs ...

Exarsi enim aliquando satiari inferis in adulescentia et siluescere ausus sum uariis et umbrosis amoribus ...[31]

---

[30]*en. Ps.* 44.9; Boulding, *Expositions* (III/16) 289.
[31]*conf.* 2.1.1; Boulding, *Confessions* (I/1) 62; CCL 27.18.

The terms *inferis* (lowly, hellish), *siluescere* (to run wild, woodsy), and *umbrosis* (shadowy, obscure) all foreshadow the pear tree and the subsequent darkness and consequent hell its violation brings about. To be filled with hell may be a way to be fed but it is no way to be satisfied.

This tricolon thus anticipates the main scene of *conf.* 2, setting the reader up nicely to understand how the pear tree scene is both the culmination of Augustine's restless adolescences as well as the iconic moment which captures all other ungodly loves. Sin is to turn away from the deified life offered to all, and instead turn to the diabolical life of one's own choosing (*illa diabolica, ista deifica*).[32] It is to find oneself torn between loving God and loving self, to run away from God (following Adam into the thicket of shame at Gen 3:10) and thus be forced to find some level of contentment in one's own shadowy self.

As we move to that scene in particular, then, we hear another descriptor for what Augustine's soul does when it turns away from God. In choosing the Latin term *dissiliens* to describe his leap downward, Augustine is picking up on a word used as the abandonment of divine unity. This is what heretics and schismatics prefer instead of the solidity of orthodox doctrine or the community of ecclesia: whereas the truth of heresy shows a hatred of God, the divisiveness of schismatics proves a hatred of neighbor.[33] Such "leaping from one place to another," *dissiliens*, stems from a desire to be cut off from community and inevitably results in division and decay. It is most often used to describe the ontological privation of evil's effects.[34] But metaphors of leaping downwards can also portray doctrinal divisions, as when Augustine and Julian of Eclanum argue that their own perceived heresy will eventually be struck downward by the truth.[35]

Such a leap is caused by an ingratitude that sees not in God but in oneself the origin of all one enjoys: "the soul will be ungrateful, if it attributes to itself what it has from God." Such a vice causes us to be "driven back (*repulsi*) from the unchangeableness of the divine substance" and we thereby fall into the disgrace of idolatry (*ad idololatriae dedecus*).[36] Discussing such idolatrous ingratitude, Augustine sees in the Apostle Paul's theology of the law in Romans 3 an admonition against those who seek to rely on their own abilities.

---

[32]*pat.* §14; CSEL 41.679.
[33]cf., *f. et symb.* 10.21.
[34]cf. *c. ep. Man.* 36.40; Teske, *The Manichean Debate* (I/19) 263.
[35]cf., *Jul op. imp.* 118.
[36]*spir. et litt.* 11.18; Teske, *Answer to the Pelagians* (I/23) 160–1.

With good reason the apostle turned from this section to mentioning with horror those who by that vice I mentioned above became empty and puffed up and who were raised up by their own efforts as if through the empty air. They did not come to rest there, but were broken and plunged downward, falling upon the statues of idols as upon rocks (*ubi non requiescerent, sed fracti dissilirent, in figmenta idolorum tamquam in lapides deciderunt*).[37]

Human pride only appears to lift one up, when in fact it is responsible for plunging the fallen even further downward. In leaping from the Father's invitation, the devil—and in reality every sinful soul—finds himself in an undesirable abasement. Pride separates while humility connects.

The stealing of pears might not be all that serious but that is precisely what the proud one wants you to believe. The enemy seeks to convince sinners that their malice is really, in the end, never too serious, as Augustine warns his flock during the Easter Octave: "the devil telling you it's only a light matter, when God tells you it is a grave one." This is, what Augustine names one of the most common ploys of the enemy, an *artificium*, that "same old ruse" (in Hill's words) which Satan used in Paradise: "it's just a tree," "it's just a piece of fruit," "it's just this one time," and we could easily fill in our own preferred lines of rationalization as well. But behind every temptation to sin is the prior temptation to think that some sins are insignificant. So, the Bishop has his hearers imagine Satan's lurking in their sins and in a quite tender way, Augustine prompts them in this way:

> "What you're doing is nothing, really; you're sinning in the flesh, after all, you're not sinning spiritually. It's something that is easily wiped off the slate, easily pardoned." What's so terrific about what he's doing [Augustine asks about Satan's tactics]? It's the same old ruse as he employed in paradise, when he said, "Eat, and you will be like gods; you certainly won't die." ...[38]

As Augustine seasons as a pastor and curator of souls, he will see that this is how the enemy of our human nature handles himself, as an angel of light and soft in suggestion. "Come on, whom are you hurting?" "Come on, who is ever going to know?" This is the "ruse" the enemy uses to try to convince

---

[37] *spir. et litt.* 12.19; Teske, *Answer to the Pelagians* (I/23) 161.
[38] *s.* 224.2; Hill, *Sermons* (III/6) 243.

us that, if even for a second, the ways of God and the community to which we supposedly belong can be suspended. We are lured above these demands and, so, behind every enticement is that ancient lie that we can become gods without God.

Augustine knows how we become what we love. "Do you love the earth? You will be earth. Do you love God? What shall I say? That you will be God? I don't dare to say this on my own ..." going on to quote Ps 82:6 and the promise (repeated at Jn 10:34) that God's followers too shall become gods.[39] The choice to become earth is entirely ours; the choice to become God's is entirely of grace and our free surrender to allowing God to indwell within each of our souls. When it comes to virtue and vice, he also knows that if we allow sins to become the nexus with which we are joined to others, that sin will become only more and more connatural to our being and we shall become more and more conformed to it:

> Surely I'm not telling you, am I, my dear brothers and sisters, that you won't be able to find any Christians leading good lives? God forbid that I should have such an opinion of my Lord's threshing floor! If that's the case, what am I slaving away for? Keep an eye out for the good people to imitate; be good yourselves, and you'll find them. But if you start being bad, you will begin to believe that they're all bad; and it's not true, you're deceiving yourselves. You're looking at the threshing floor from a distance, that's why only the chaff strikes you. Come nearer, look, fill your hands, apply the judgment of your breath; everything that is light and can fly is blown out of your hands, and what is heavy remains .... Like meets like. Are you a grain? You attach yourselves to grains. Are you chaff? You attach yourself to chaff.[40]

This is how that evening years ago seemingly began: Augustine had joined himself to chaff, to those "nasty lads" who were united around not the good but around the thrill of exerting their own wills, regardless what the night brought.

(5) Pear pressure?

This is why as the images and insights of the pear tree scene unfold, next comes Augustine's admittance that it was the reality of community that

---

[39]ep. Jo. 2.14; Ramsey, *Homilies on the First Epistle of* John (I/14) 51.
[40]s. 260D.2; Hill, *Sermons* (III/7) 204.

enticed him to do what he did. In fact, this reality of traveling and acting in a pack is the closest we come to receiving an answer into why Augustine stole pears he found neither enticing nor needed to sate some hunger. Notice, therefore, how he does not immediately provide a simple motive for this relatively innocuous action. He is truly unable.

He therefore first canvasses what I believe to be three, not explanations but, results of this deed. As we shall see, the explanation is nonsensical, a paradox so vacuous that it can hardly be described. The closest we get to a rational explanation is the youthful desire for camaraderie, the need to "fit in" and be one of the group. Before we hear of that, though, Augustine first admits that (1) some of the pears were thrown to the pigs, but that is not why they stole them; (2) some were eaten, but that is not why they stole them; and (3) the pears may have gone untroubled, Augustine admits, if he had been wandering by that garden alone. "I most certainly would not have done it alone." This confession is the closest we have to an intelligible reason, an efficient cause, for why our saint-in-the-making does something he regrets so woefully later. But even this, it seems to me, is not laid down as the definitive explanation for this theft. Community and acting as one of many did, however, sweeten the crime.

Augustine knew how we are not the individualistic, self-made men and women we pride ourselves to be; instead, we are the result of so much "group think," learning what it is we want from observing those wanting and choosing around us. Is Augustine here painting himself as a human Satan, one who sought to alleviate his own fallenness by alluring others into his divine aversion? Could Eve have seen the Tree of the Knowledge of Good and Evil as "good for food and pleasing to the eyes" (Gen 3:6) before Satan had pointed it out to her (Gen 3:1)? We may never know but German philologist and philosopher Eric Auerbach (d. 1957) wants us to see that when we follow another intent on godlessness we end up losing even our own selves.

Using the example of Alypius at the games at *conf.* 6.8.13, Auerbach points out how vice depersonalizes and defaces those who truly turn to it. Remember how Alypius had sworn off the games and, relying on his own strength and ability to keep his eyes closed at the sounds of the sanguineous stadium, he allows his friends to drag him into the games. At the cry of some otherwise undescribed carnage, Alypius let go of his resolve, opened his eyes and "fell more dreadfully than the other man whose fall had evoked the shouting." As such, he found himself no longer as a man who had attended the games. Instead, "No longer was he the man who had joined the crowd; he was now one of the crowd he had joined, and a genuine companion of those who had led him there."[41] In his 1953 classic *Mimesis*, Auerbach examines the convergence of acting in a group and the result of vice or virtue in Augustine. Predating the mimetic theory of René Girard (d. 2015), Auerbach sees how derivative desire is at the root of so much of our supposed self-determination:

> So Alypius is not overly concerned when he is dragged by comradely coercion into the amphitheater. He trusts in his closed eyes and his determined will. But his proud individualistic self-reliance is overwhelmed in no time. And it is not merely a random Alypius whose pride, nay whose inmost being, is thus crushed: it is the entire rational individualistic culture of classical antiquity: Plato and Aristotle, the Stoa and Epicurus. A burning lust has swept them away, in one powerful assault ['Nor was he now the same as he came in, but was one of the throng into which he came']. The individual, the man of noble self reliance, the man who chooses for himself, despiser of excesses, has become one of the mass.[42]

While the enervation of proud Rome is captured so skillfully here, as one of the great subcurrents running throughout the Confessions, well exemplified when the great Latin orator Marius Victorinus turns from the ways of his old Roman clan to be washed in the waters of his new Catholic family—"Rome stood amazed, while the Church was jubilant."[43] Unlike Alypius, Victorinus's name is announced over and over publicly in the halls of his new home. Where there is conversion toward the good, there is jubilation; where there is perversion into sin, lies degradation. Victorinus's surrendering allows his individuality to be perfected and thus proclaimed; whereas Alypius's deprivation drags him faceless into the crowd, objectified into oblivion. Virtue perfects, vice defects.

The social anomy and false companions Augustine can detect only later stand in contrast to the Church and the real community forged there alone. John Cavadini makes the excellent point that the one thing pride demands is praise, and without an audience, Augustine's pride would go unnoticed, unappreciated. In this way, writes Cavadini, "Augustine's little band of young

---

[41]*conf.* 6.8.13; Boulding, *Confessions* (I/1) 146.
[42]Eric Auerbach, *Mimesis: The Representation of Reality in Western Literature* (Princeton: Princeton University Press [1953] 1991) 69.
[43]*conf.* 8.2.3-.5; Boulding, *Confessions* (I/1) 188.

thieves becomes an image of the sinful fellowship of Adam and Eve ..."[44]
This is a crucial aspect of the scene Scott MacDonald likewise emphasizes
that the theft of pears was Augustine's way of being "in love with loving,"
his one desire at *conf.* 3.1.1. This misdeed becomes the way he can find
affirmation from his peers: "Augustine shows us how the theft of the pears,
too, can be understood as a misguided and disordered attempt at loving and
being loved."[45] As helpful as these veteran Augustinian mentors are here,
I hold that the communal aspect—as important as it is to understanding
the scene—does not wholly account for an explanation. There is something
more at work here than just bad teenaged company.

The tragic allure of nothingness: Loving evil pe(a)r se?

Of all the possible reasons given in the narrative—(1) throwing the fruit
to the pigs, (2) eating a few, and (3) the importance of community—on
why Augustine did what he did that dark summer eve, none stand up fully
to his scrutiny. In fact, throughout this scene, Augustine actually raises
fourteen possible reasons this may have been done: pride, honors and glory,
ferocity, flirtatiousness, curiosity, ignorance or stupidity, sloth, lush living,
extravagance, avarice, envy, anger, timidity, and sadness.[46] As important as
these vices are to detect in one's soul, there is something more, something
much more dastardly than any of these. No one of these deficiencies can
satisfy Augustine's explanation of the theft. In fact, there is no obvious goal
of this theft, no apparent advantage to be gained in this garden. That is why
this evening shines brightly in Augustine's mind so many years later. He is
retrospectively wondering why he experienced such exhilaration from such
disorder. What strikes him initially about this dissonance in his soul is that
he sought no real good in pilfering the pears.

---

[44]Cavadini, "Book Two: Augustine's Book of Shadows," *A Reader's Guide to Augustine's Confessions*, 33.

[45]MacDonald, "Petit Larceny, The Beginning of All Sin: Augustine's Theft of the Pears," *Augustine's Confessions: Critical Essays*, 45–69; 57. This phrase was surely lifted from the *Catiline Orations* of Cicero (at 2.23) where Cicero is describing Catiline's cronies as profligate youth who have learned how to cause mayhem and are concerned only about *amare et amari*, loving and being loved.

[46]All of these occur in *conf.* 2.6.13; Boulding, *Confessions* (I/1) 44–5.

Different from other crimes, Augustine and his cronies were not pursuing some external good, however wrongly. Those who perpetuated the crime sought nothing outside the crime. That is why Augustine next introduces malfeasances with which the just person may disagree but which are intelligible precisely because there is at least some good sought, and a motive can therefore be given: homicide for the sake of taking a man's wife or estate, the conspirator Catiline's attempt to overthrow the Roman Republic in order to secure greater prestige and propel his own power:

> Suppose someone has committed homicide. Why did he do it? Perhaps he was in love with the victim's wife, or coveted his estate, or wanted to steal from him in order to support himself, or feared to be robbed of the like himself by the other man, or had been injured and burned for revenge. Is it likely that he would kill another person without any motive, simply because he enjoyed killing? Who could believe that? ... Even Catiline, then, did not love his criminal acts for their own sake, but only the advantages he had in view when committing them.[47]

When examining evil acts, we can usually discern some reason, some sought after good or gain, for acting the way one does. The murderer seeks his neighbor's wife; Cataline seeks political power; the glutton desires simply another mouthful; and so on.

As horrendous as some evils are, these types of actions are rather easy to discern ethically. But in that dark garden, something else occurred. Augustine became a thief for no gain, for no stealth savoring. He committed a crime simply because the thrill of going against the good, allured by the total opposite of the good—privation—was enticing. Even the bloodthirsty who long for the Roman games are after something they desire and can easily name:

> The charioteers compete for some prize; for what prize do the crowds fight over the charioteers? But the charioteer delights them, the hunter delights them, the player delights them. Is this the way it is, then, that vile baseness delights the decent man? You know you can also change your consuming addiction to shows and spectacles; the Church is offering your mind more honest and venerable spectacles.[48]

---

[47]*conf.* 2.5.11; Boulding, *Confessions* (I/1) 69.
[48]*s.* 313A.3; Hill, *Sermons* (III/9) 92.

But Augustine's theft was different, unlike the common sins where one chooses a lower good over one higher; he came to realize that he was ultimately after nothing. Even the vile man—the adulterer, the murderer and even the political usurper—can tell you why he did what he did. But if evil is truly nothing, *priuatio boni*, how can nothing allure? How can a privation attract? It cannot and that is why the pear tree stands as something indelible on Augustine's soul so many years after the fact.

For although the object of his juvenile thievery, a few pears, may be enormously less than the life of a man or the welfare of a state, this action continues to gnaw at Augustine's psyche. He remains haunted for having entered deeply into the mystery of iniquity, "deriving pleasure from the deed" because he was in love with his own ruin (*amaui perire*), and not because of some benefit gained. He relished the act for no other reason that "it was forbidden." There was no good he sought, only the exertion of his own will. No good to be possessed, no sweetness to be enjoyed, only the thrill of his own assertion of self. There was no reason, and that is why he came to find himself *gratis malus*. Herein lies Augustine's aporia: he has become "bad for no reason." What could this mean? How is one to make moral progress or grow in sanctity if one cannot give a reason why seeking union with God does not attract, if even momentarily? But as he knew when inquiring into the rebellion of Lucifer, to look for an efficient cause of an evil will is pointless. Only a deficient cause can be given and one wonders what that even means.

Augustine warns that it is fruitless to seek the efficient cause of an evil will (*efficientem causam malae uoluntatis*), for it is like trying to see the dark or trying to listen attentively to silence.[49] Yet, here under the pear tree, Augustine experienced a tenebrous maliciousness for no real reason. *Malus gratis.* Is there sheer gratuitousness at both ends of the moral and existential spectrum? As we learn from his interaction later with the Pelagians, God bestows his grace to some for no reason—*bonus gratis*?—and here at the bottom of life's moments, Augustine became unexplainably wicked. Is there a divine gratuitousness as well as an evil one? The only motive (*causa*) he is able to discern was the malice (*malitia*) of his own disgracefulness: "The malice was loathsome, and I loved it. I was in love with my own ruin, in love with decay" (*Foeda erat, et amaui eam; amaui perire, amaui defectum meum*).[50] The defective reality sought here cannot be a mere absence but a frustrated, and frustrating, nothing–something.

---

[49]*ciu. Dei* 12.7: "No one, therefore, should look for an efficient cause for an evil will ... like wanting to see darkness or hear silence."; Babcock, *City of God* (I/7) 43; CCL 47.362.
[50]*conf.* 2.4.9; CCL 27.22.

In one of the Cassiciacum dialogues (late 386/early 387), *On The Happy Life*, our Christian catechumen is still pondering the paradoxical power of evil to allure. In this early work evil is defined as a wickedness (*nequitia*), a sort of "not anything" (*nec quicquam*). It is not a mere nothing, but it is not really anything to which one could point to or define. Nonetheless, this iniquity is the "mother of all defects" (*matrem omnium uitiorum*). So as not to leave his readers thinking that something as crucial as the source of all evil is a stasis easily put aside, here the young Augustine goes on to describe such nihil as "… a wickedness from sterility, that is from nothing. Nothing is whatever is flowing, dissolving, melting, and—so to speak—constantly perishing. Hence we call such persons lost (*perditos*)."[51] The source of all evil then is a mysterious iniquity from which all other perdition comes. It is the possibility of turning away from God and thus living life not as God wills but in the wretchedness of our own aversion from the *beata uita* offered us.

As a shadowy nothing, evil has the ability to woo the fallen soul. But how can nothingness provide any real answer since it cannot be the efficient cause of our sinning? The answer may not be all too satisfying but there is no efficient cause but only a deficient cause, this becoming "bad for no reason." Or, as we read later in *ciu. Dei*, evil is a defection and a turning from God (*defectus … ab opere Dei*) which renders "the works of the will evil because they were willed according to the self and not according to God."[52] Again, we see this consistently in Augustine's thought: turn toward God and become like him, flourishing and enjoying all that God has made; turn away from God and trust in yourself, you will know only fragmentation and dissolution. This is what evil is for Augustine, perhaps a no-thing but some sort of verity all the same. That is, it is something that we must properly acknowledge and understand; nihil is not the sort of metaphysical factor that can simply be disregarded. It is something that must be discerned rightly so as not to be allured by it. As we have seen, Augustine was spending those peaceful months of retreat in Cassiciacum reviewing his past life and pondering the meaning of his fast-approaching baptism. As he looked back, he admitted that the uninformed and spiritually lazy are in fact drawn by this shadowy no-thing. By being ignorant of nihil (along with formless matter, space and time, and other metaphysical categories), one "will fall into all possible types of errors."[53]

---

[51]*b. uit.* 2.8; CCL 29.70.
[52]*ciu. Dei* 14.11; Babcock, *City of God* (I/7) 116.
[53]*ord.* 2.16.44; *On Order*, trans., Silvano Borruso (South Bend: St. Augustine's Press, 2007) 109.

Think of an author typing these words. Each word is intelligible to you, the reader, because there is a blank space in between each. Is there not a *no-thing* separating each word and, in fact, each letter as well? However, if the reader were to become bedazzled by this space, this no-thing, and consequently fail to pay attention to the sensible word, then any reader would get caught up in the what-is-not instead of turn toward the what-is, an author's writing would become fragmented and nonsensical. Is this why the pear tree scene still haunts Augustine? Is it the closest he ever got to nothingness? Is he wrestling with the paradox that in his shallow youth and ignorance, he allowed "nothing" to allure him and he gladly fell headlong?

Modern commentators on Augustine have examined this connection between the allure of evil and the actual nothingness which we only retrospectively seek. For example, Mary Clark noticed this phenomenon and linked it explicitly with the nonbeing that attracts when we sin for no real gain but only for the thrill of rejecting the ultimate. "There are decisions for nonbeing, made by persons created ex nihilo with openness to Absolute Being. Augustine confessed to making such decisions himself until through God's providence he found in Christ, the Word made flesh, the exemplar of all humanness and the Logos through whom all things are made and made valuable."[54] The human creature exists from God *ex nihil* and this wholly imbalanced pair remains a constant tension in the lives of those on their pilgrim way: the decision for God or nothingness. Only the Absolute's entry into the created order can grant creatures ultimate value, but until one is willing to unite the disjointed with the whole, one will continue to slash himself with these sharp edges of good but fragmented creatures.

This is how the popular religion writer Garry Wills describes the Augustinian psychology of sin as well, as "an introduction of no-being into the created order by the will's abandonment of greater goods to slide down toward lesser ones, those with less existence where there should have been more."[55] Hereafter the goods of creation, says Wills, become a torture because fallen souls can never have the eternity for which they were created on their own terms. Enjoying the deepest desires of one's heart ironically means to surrender all to the Love of God. This is precisely what the self-centered refuse to do. Their "nothingness" in comparison to God's "everything" thus continues to beckon and hold sway over their distorted attempts at self-

---

[54]Mary Clark, *Augustine* (London: Geoffrey Chapman, 1994) 107.
[55]Garry Wills, *Saint Augustine's Sin* (New York: Viking Books, 2003) 11.

deification; in this aversion away from God's glory into the murkiness of self, inveterate disappointments are formed. That is, when one thinks only about one's sins and not the Lord's goodness, the sinner perceives himself to be so lost, the only option he thinks he has is to continue in the ways which have grown familiar to him. This place Augustine calls a "certain depth" (*quale profundum*) because out of it an identity has been formed; malicious and ultimately not true, but an identity all the same.

> Someone knows himself to be overwhelmed by daily sins, crushed beneath heaped-up loads of iniquity, and he is urged to offer supplications to God. He ridicules the idea (*irridet*). How does he reply? First he says, "If my villainies were offensive to God, would I be left alive? If God concerned himself with human actions, would I, with all the crimes I have committed, not only be still alive but even prospering?"[56]

For dramatic effect, this question is put in the mouth of a fictitious interlocutor by our preacher, but the query itself is ancient. This is the same doubt Eve herself was tempted to in the garden. "Now the snake was the most cunning of all the wild animals that the Lord God had made. He asked the woman, 'Did God really say, "You shall not eat from any of the trees in the garden"'?" (Gen 3:1). Assured of her own power, Eve questions God's veracity and instead trusts "her own independent authority and a certain proud overconfidence in herself."[57] Augustine depicts this drama in Eden as a creature trusting her own experience—for Eve does not (immediately) die upon eating the fruit—over the Creator's own promises. For, in fact, she does see that the tree looks far too lovely to be dangerous and encourages Adam to do the same. This is the foretaste of hell: to prefer one's own supposed surety over the relationship of trust God himself offers.

This is precisely what Augustine thinks those who move from vice to vice choose to do: they allow themselves to be fooled that their choices will not result in anything unfortunate, and in their immediate success(es) they continue to fall deeper and deeper into a world of deception. Augustine thus continues his gloss on Psalm 129:

> This is what happens to people deeply sunk in sin: they are successful in their wrongdoing, and plunge yet deeper in the measure that they regard

---

[56]*en. Ps.* 129.1; Boulding, *Expositions* (III/20) 128.
[57]*Gn. litt.* 11.13.39; Hill, *Genesis* (I/13) 451.

themselves as lucky. Illusory fortune is in truth a greater misfortune. Then such persons proceed to another argument: "I have already committed innumerable sins, and damnation awaits me. So why should I let slip the chance to do all the bad things in my power?" This is the attitude adopted by desperate robbers: "If the judge is going to execute me for ten murders in exactly the same way as for five, or even for one, why shouldn't I do whatever I like?" This is what scripture means by the words, *A person devoid of reverence goes deep into sin and is defiant.*[58]

Since I have already sinned, Augustine's pastoral advice realizes, what is one more fall, one more binge, one more rush? If I am already "used goods," why not continue to destroy myself through my sin and decay? If I have already had one too many, what's one more?

From his own lived experience early on, as well as his later priestly care for so many others, Augustine deeply realizes that when "a sinner has plumbed such depths, he is defiant. In what sense? He no longer believes in any divine providence; or, if he does believe in it, he does not think it extends to himself. He gives himself unrestrained license to sin; having lost hope of pardon, he gives free rein to iniquity."[59] Even the stoniest of sinners realizes that his vice is destroying something beautiful and he figures he is now out of God's grace. If that God refuses me, I must therefore become my own god. As such, I can now grant myself "unrestrained license" (*peccandi licentiam*) to do whatever I desire, and to destroy what the other supposedly does not want. For here there is no hope of reform, no promise of pardon, and surely no peace at the ready.

This Augustinian insight, that turning away from God's providence only fosters my own self-destruction, was captured in a twentieth-century criminological study named *The Broken Window Theory*. A well-known experiment in social geography, *The Broken Window* experiment became a metaphor for the direct link between isolation and destruction. In 1969 a Stanford University psychologist by the name of Philip Zimbardo sought to record this connection by placing similar automobiles in both a seedy section of the Bronx as well as in the affluent city of Palo Alto, CA. The hood of each car was left up, the license plate of each car was ripped off, and all obvious signs of ownership or care were removed from sight. Within ten

---

[58]*en. Ps.* 129.1; Boulding, *Expositions* (III/20) 128.
[59]*en. Ps.* 142.13; Boulding, *Expositions* (III/20) 355.

minutes, we learn, the car in the Bronx began to be stripped and within twenty-four hours, the automobile was entirely ransacked and left on blocks. It is no surprise that the car not far from sunny Stanford went unmolested for more than a week. But once Zimbardo took it upon himself to begin to smash the car with a sledgehammer under the cover of darkness, it too became a communal object of looting and destruction.

In 1982 James Wilson and George Kelling published a popular version of this study in *The Atlantic Monthly*, arguing that if a window is broken in a given neighborhood or automobile, other destructive actions inevitably not only occur but even explode and proliferate. When brokenness is apparent, perpetrators gain confidence that their actions will go unnoticed and violence increases. Wilson and Kelling also applied this to interpersonal relationships and a police officer's interaction with men loitering in the street. In interactions where those idling were called by name and proper respect was shown to them by genuine questions of concern, harmony and reconciliation were a common result. In those interactions where people felt bullied and harassed, objectified and seen as a nuisance, on the other hand, hostilities arose: "Untended property becomes fair game for people out for fun or plunder ... Because of the nature of community life in the Bronx—its anonymity, the frequency with which cars are abandoned and things are stolen or broken, the past experience of 'no one caring'—vandalism begins much more quickly than it does in staid Palo Alto."[60] This probably does not surprise us, and this is Augustine's point when looking back at the pears: when feeling invaded and broken, the fallen soul likewise tends to destroy itself through further failings. Sin destroys and destruction leads to loathing; in turn, self-loathing leads to more destruction, and eventually the beaten and bruised simply want to disappear.

Augustine makes this point in many ways but in one clever sermon, he has his congregation imagine a disgruntled monk who, turning against his recently embraced vocation, leaves the brothers in disgust. Having been hurt by what he judges to be an injustice committed by such so-called brothers, the ex-monk grows even more hateful and intolerant.

---

[60]George L. Kelling and James Q. Wilson, "Broken Windows: The Police and Neighborhood Safety," *The Atlantic Monthly* 249:3 (March 1982) 29–38; 31. These same points are made throughout John T. Cacioppo and William Patrick's study, *Loneliness: Human Nature and the Need for Social Connection* (New York: W. W. Norton & Co., 2008), e.g., "Those who felt depressed withdrew from others and became lonelier over time. So here too was the stop-and-go mechanism of loneliness and depressive symptoms we had postulated, working in opposition to create a pernicious cycle of learned helplessness and passive coping" (90–1).

Remember that they must be tolerated for a while in the hope of their being reformed, and they cannot easily be expelled unless they have been given the chance of being tolerated first. Our newcomer, however, is impatient and in no mood for tolerance. "Who lured me into this place? I thought there would be charity here!" Exasperated by the tiresome habits of a few he abandons his holy resolve, and, since he has not persevered in what he promised, he becomes guilty of a broken vow. Moreover, having left the community he too becomes a scurrilous scandal-monger … What is worse, by belching out the bad smell of his resentment he frightens away others who would enter, because though he did enter himself, he lacked the strength to persevere. "What kind of people are they?" he asks. "Jealous, disputatious, intolerant, miserly! One of the community did such-and-such, and another something else just as nasty …" You bad fellow, why pass over the good ones in silence? You parade the people you could not put up with, but say nothing of those who put up with your own bad ways.[61]

One sin leads to another. Frustration in one's asceticism leads to disruptions into the community, to a broken vow, to the spreading of gossip. From the self-imposed isolation of one sinner, an entire religious house is affected and, in turn, the wider society has its trust shaken in what they once perceived to be a holy ecclesia.

Paul Rigby has masterfully assessed Augustine on self-loathing and points out there are three distinct moments in this deadly cycle of sin: (1) the privation the evil effects, (2) the emptiness the sinner inevitably senses, and (3) the self-hatred which is the response of having ruined one's wholeness. In hating the good, we hate God and in hating God we inevitably hate those made in God's image: Augustine "is trapped, for he hates God and himself, and the more he hates God the less he has what he wants and consequently the more he dislikes himself. Privation leads to emptiness and emptiness leads to self-hatred."[62] This is what the pear tree showed Augustine that infamous evening: to grasp after satisfaction apart from the only one who can satisfy ensnares and turns one in on oneself. This is the disappointment and the loathing of the self which every reflective sinner knows. Rigby thus continues:

---

[61]*en. Ps.* 99.12; Boulding, *Expositions* (III/19) 24.
[62]Paul Rigby, *The Theology of Augustine's Confessions* (Cambridge: Cambridge University Press, 2015) 113.

> Augustine uncovers the positive power of evil. Triple hatred [i.e., God, truth, self] gives the motive force that made Augustine stand up in arrogance before God in Book 2 of the *Confessions*. Sham omnipotence, friendship unfriendly, shame and fear of exposure, though they are "nothing," derive their power from the posited choice of triple hatred, which Augustine discovers as already there. Hatred of God is invincible because it is tied to hatred of truth. This double hatred surfaces only as a self-severing exercise that perverts the search for true happiness and issues in self-hatred. Self-hatred itself is recognized consciously only as dissatisfied self-love.[63]

Malformed desires lead to the pride of self-divinization. Made in the divine image, I cannot help but want to become divine. But two things call me, two possible realities stretch my divided heart: God and the nihil from which God brought me. Of course, no one can be wooed by nothing, but such nothingness can appear attractive to the sinful soul, for in this blank space I find the void to become my own sovereign, a power unto myself. This is what Augustine calls a perverse love of self. It is a choosing for oneself that which only appears to be good but is cyclically destructive, which as we shall see next, is ultimately revealed as self-hatred.

Conclusion

When examining a relatively harmless offense of his teenage years, Augustine admits that this deed remains worthy of confession because it was as close to the abyss of nothingness as he could wander. He sought to destroy himself because at least *he* was the one doing it. Such ruin attracts our divided selves because now the demands of goodness are dismissed, and the riskiness of relationship is relinquished. Once in the light, the converted Augustine came to see that what he was choosing was not the specious beauty of the pears themselves, but was instead choosing his own self as the source of his security. Augustine, not the pears, had become the idol which had to be shattered.

Augustine's intention in stealing the pears was never to satisfy his physical hunger, but to deepen the crevice of self-loathing that had already fractured

---

[63]Rigby, *op. cit.*, 114.

his heart. Still unwilling to confess that God has calibrated his beauty to Augustine's brokenness, our searcher refused to place himself in God's pierced hands. He instead relished his own decay, sweetening it all the more through senseless acts of ruin. But through this self-imposed alienation, God continued to call and call all the more loudly. Augustine's psychology of sin reveals the depths of the double minded soul. In sin we are alienated against our own selves because we are both drawn to and repulsed by goodness. Augustine is clearly no longer a Manichean who abhors all visible creation. As a Christian he sees all the more clearly the beauty of everything that meets his senses; but as a sinner he is also disgusted by anything that demands his allegiance. He wants to embrace the other but must first learn that he is sought, wanted. This is the risk of relationship, of letting ourselves be known, healed, and loved. This is where we cease ravishing our ruin and allow our ruin to be ravished by the one who alone promises true rest.

Augustine is the first Christian to chronicle such rebellion. In sinning, we ultimately tell God to vanish, to leave us alone. But in so doing, we eventually realize we were forcing ourselves to disappear. We cannot help but love, but when we fall in love with what is unlovable, we inevitably fall "in love with [our] own ruin, in love with decay." And whereas every lover is famished, Augustine admits the same sense of craving—not for a beloved, but simply "hungering for ... foulness itself." The pear tree scene becomes symbolic for Augustine because it represents our desire to choose nothingness itself, to find contentment in the only true rival to God.

But what he alerted us to in a way no one has since is the loathing and destruction of our own selves. Why is it, that at a very profound depth, we simply do not want to be whole? Why do I overeat even though I know it is not going to make me feel good in the long run? Why do I insist on lying and gossiping when I know these words which come out of my mouth are only going to imprison me later? Why do I continually embrace thoughts and actions that I know will not make me feel better about myself? Why are we intent upon our own destruction? In his misguided drive for wholeness, Augustine relied on himself to make his truest self disappear, thus confessing how he used sin to destroy himself. Freely behaving recklessly, he sought to ruin any good he sensed within himself. This is something every sinner knows: my sinful actions may not provide for me the best possible reality, but at least it is *my* reality.

CHAPTER 4
NARCISSISM AND THE PARADOX OF SELF-LOVE

> "Amy was very, very wary of me," Faithfull said.
> "She knew that I knew and she didn't want me to say anything.
> There's a level of narcissism which is all mixed up with self-hatred.
> I know it well."[1]

The proper love of self is the key to unlocking the mystery of Christian love. We will not be able to be entrusted with community until we learn this lesson rightly: "First see if you yet know how to love yourself; and then I will entrust your neighbor to you, whom you are to love as yourself. But if you don't yet know how to love yourself, I'm afraid you are only too likely to cheat your neighbor as yourself."[2] Made for communion, we cannot help but reach out and love. Augustine was a seasoned enough pastor, however, to know that while we must love, we can very easily love wrongly. When we allow only ourselves into that God-given image and likeness, created and given for another, the result will always be, in one form or another, self-hatred. In fact, he knew well that the Great Christian Commandment instructs us to love only two others, our God and our neighbor as ourselves (Mk 12:3-31; Mt 22:36-40).[3] As such, there is no law to love oneself because it seemingly occurs automatically. "No one can hate his own flesh" (Eph 5:29), Paul tells the Church at Ephesus, but this is something Augustine would have earlier learned from his first intellectual mentor. As Cicero's reflections on the natural law maintained, taking care of oneself rightly is part and parcel of being a creature:

---

[1] Marianne Faithfull on her friendship with the singer Amy Winehouse who overdosed at the age of twenty-seven at the height of her career in a 2011 interview in *Rolling Stone Magazine*, as reported at www.cnn.com/2014/08/06/showbiz/celebrity-news-gossip/marianne-faithfull-boyfriend-jim-morrison-rs/index.html.

[2] *s.* 128.5; Hill, *Sermons* (III/4) 295.

[3] Cf., *f. inuis.* 2.4.

That immediately upon birth (for that is the proper point to start from) a living creature feels an attachment for itself, and an impulse to preserve itself and to feel affection for its own constitution and for those things which tend to preserve that constitution; while on the other hand it conceives an antipathy to destruction and to those things which appear to threaten destruction. In proof of this opinion they urge that infants desire things conducive to their health and reject things that are the opposite before they have ever felt pleasure or pain; this would not be the case, unless they felt an affection for their own constitution and were afraid of destruction. But it would be impossible that they should feel desire at all unless they possessed self-consciousness, and consequently felt affection for themselves. This leads to the conclusion that it is love of self which supplies the primary impulse to action.[4]

Cicero obviously averred that all living things inescapably seek out their own preservation and cannot do otherwise. All creatures that breathe and move enjoy an innate affection for themselves and eschew anything that brings about their destruction. Self-love, it would thus seem, is the first step in experiencing what it is to be alive.

If these pages were highlighting the thought of Augustine the philosophically trained rhetorician only, this Ciceronian claim would appear axiomatic, as the basis of Roman natural law was self-preservation. But there is another strand of thought at work here. Augustine the Christianized catechumen came to teach that self-love is exactly what brought about the fall and ruin of all humankind: "*Prima hominis perditio, fuit amor sui.*"[5] Something new regarding self-love has obviously snuck into his intellectual maturation. Now *amor sui* is no longer the bestowed instinct in all living creatures, as found in Cicero; in the later mind of Augustine it is now called out as a fragile two-faced precariousness. It can be what saves an existent from losing itself but it can also be how one does in fact lose him or herself. This is what Augustine the Christian fears: that those creatures endowed with free will cannot not love themselves, but that they will love themselves

---

[4]Cicero, *De Finibus* 3.5.16, trans., H. Harris Rackham (Cambridge, MA: Harvard University Press, Loeb Classical Series, 1931) 234–5.

[5]*s.* 96.2; Hill, *Sermons* (III/4) 29–30: "Man's first ruin was caused by love of self. I mean, if he hadn't loved himself, and had put God before himself, he would have wanted always to be subject to God, and he wouldn't have turned away to disregarding God's will and doing his own."

wrongly. So, if self-love is primal and supposedly natural to all things, how can *amor sui* be so cosmically perditious? This is the question this chapter aims to clarify. If our overall aim is to understand sin as a form of self-sabotage, at some point along the way we must take up Augustine's insistence that while one cannot not love oneself, one can love oneself wrongly which is tantamount to a form of self-hatred and thus destruction.

To work out Augustine's rather complicated thinking on this matter, this chapter proceeds first by way of sketching out his understanding of love of self. The theme of proper self-love runs through much of what Augustine has to say about the two great commands, love of God and love of neighbor, and we shall encapsulate his rich theology of charity. The second theme leads us into the extreme form of improper love of self. While Augustine never used the myth of Narcissus to explain the dangers of *amor sui*, the many themes contained in the story of Ovid (which the boy Augustine surely read) and the aporiae of the Augustinian love of self converge in a rich and illuminating manner. Our third section takes up the self-harm that inevitably arises from a misplaced love of self, a form of idolization that results in the ruin of misplaced loves. In our desire for love we erect idols of all sorts. In our realization of emptiness, we eventually tear them down, and the thrill of this destruction drew Augustine to the abyss of nothingness. This is what the alienation of trying to love oneself without loving the other brings about: isolation and then destruction.

The paradox of self-love

As Augustine sees it, those made in the image and likeness of love cannot not love. We are inevitably drawn to love. Never dwelling on any possible differences between *caritas, dilectio*, or *amor*, Augustine must not have seen any real importance in choosing one of those words for love over any other. Various metaphors and similes for love abound throughout Augustine's corpus—it is like feet (*pedes*) or wings (*alae*)—almost always having to do with an ecstatic movement carrying the lover through this journey of life. It is perhaps most famously the weight that draws any lover toward his or her beloved: *pondus meum, amor meus*.[6] But in our fallen state we must receive and thus reply to love rightly. No human person merely wants to exist, each wishes a life of blessedness, a life of loving and being loved, and love of self

---

[6]*conf.* 13.9.10; CCL 27.246.

is the beginning of such a happy life: "... for he who loves himself wants nothing other than to be happy (*non enim qui se diligit aliud uult esse quam beatus*)."[7] The problem is that there are many simulacra of love and the first and most dangerous is a wrongly ordered love of self. For to love oneself wrongly for Augustine is actually to hate oneself and where there is such neglecting, destruction is close behind.

This is why Bishop Augustine exhorts his flock to look deeply into their hearts to discern what love is truly Christ's and where the world has instilled fictions of true charity. True to his Christian anthropology, he does not waste time asking if his congregants love. Of course they do. The real question for authentic growth, then, becomes where are you loving rightly and where do you love wrongly? This is what must be discerned, as our pastor's worry for his people is that they allow themselves to love on their own terms and not on Christ's:

> If, however, you love yourself in yourself, even though you are not vexed within yourself by any kind of greedy desire (and who would ever dare really to make such a boast?), and are therefore very pleased with yourself, the very fact that you are afraid of nothing is something that should give you cause for even more serious alarm. You see, it isn't with any sort of love that fear has to be cast out, but with the upright kind of love with which we love God totally, and our neighbor with the intention that he may love God that way too. But to love oneself in oneself and thus to be very pleased with oneself, is not the justice of charity, but the pride of vanity. And that's why the apostle was quite right to lash out with his rebukes (1 Tim 3:1–5) at those who love themselves and are very pleased with themselves.[8]

Loving oneself rightly is actually not to be pleased (*se ipsos amantes et sibi placentes*) with oneself, as if that self could actually love without being first in loving communion with Love. This is the Augustinian paradox: that to love oneself means first to reach out of oneself, to display a movement away from oneself because one realizes that alone the self is horribly insufficient and defective. We are made for the communion that enables us to love ourselves by first loving God and neighbor. "By loving God, he also loves himself, so that he may love his neighbor as himself with the love that leads

---

[7] *ciu. Dei* 10.3; Babcock, *City of God* (I/6) 308; CCL 47.275.
[8] *s.* 348.2; Hill, *Sermons* (III/10) 92.

to salvation."[9] If there is a love that leads to salvation, there must be a love that leads to destruction.

This is the goal of good discernment: to sift truly through the desires of one's heart to separate the only true love from the false loves which only masquerade as charity. The former turns out to be God's very nature and in turn becomes his gift to his beloved; the latter are revealed as all the various imposters of charity we can all too easily entertain all lifelong. To distinguish these two competitors, we need to journey within, to find the love of God already poured into our hearts, (Rom 5:5 being Augustine's most often quoted biblical verse).[10] This is because true love is never manufactured by a creature. When we understand love as Augustine does, we recall that love is neither a feeling nor an emotion. Following the Evangelist, Augustine insists that we understand love to be God's very essence—*Deus caritas est* (1 Jn 4:8). As such, authentic charity can come only from God and be directed only back to God—*caritas ex Deo* (1 Jn 4:7). So, while there are many impostors of love in our lives—lust, control, manipulation, the inordinate desire to be noticed and wanted, and so on—once we realize what a prodigal giver the Triune God is, we are able to overcome the fear of searching our souls, knowing that he is present only as love. Augustine's pastoral sensitivity is one that stresses the love of God over all things. This is a love that demands not our self-assurance, however, but a love that asks for our surrender, that deep, humbling realization that alone we are moribund. Where we feel self-assured, we inevitably keep out all others. This is the beginning of our self-imposed alienations and exactly how Augustine the pastor will attack sin and show others how to let themselves realize the love of God which defeats all destruction.

This is why he preaches that we need never fear the mutual indwelling Christ desires. Before Love himself, we need not rely on impressing him with undue flattery, nor need we feel ashamed before him. Both are obvious tendencies for the fallen soul: on the one hand to wear one's successes and strengths for the world to see, while all the time knowing one's own fragility and weaknesses. Augustine, however, has his congregants imagine Jesus standing directly in the middle of this cacophony. Before him one need not try to impress or win over; before him one need not retreat shamefaced. Christ comes into his people simply to show them their truest selves. This is

---

[9] *en. Ps.* 118, *exp.* 27.6; Boulding, *Expositions* (III/19) 474.
[10] The classic here is still Anne-Marie La Bonnardière, "Le verset paulinien Rom., v. 5 dans l'oeuvre de saint Augustin," *Augustinus Magister* 2 (1954) 657–65.

the self that strives more and more for perfect surrender, not being satisfied with itself but knowing that true life comes only through properly ordered charity.

To avoid self-destruction we must therefore learn to love ourselves rightly, and for Augustine this means ordering our loves appropriately. The *ordo amoris* is realizing how even though the love of neighbor and self is chronologically and emotionally prior, the love of God must be ontologically and authoritatively primary. By definition, then, love is never in competition with love. Yet, for this cohesion to occur, the proper ordering of love must occur: one's love of God must be the defining and unifying *telos* by which all other loves are informed. The Bishop of Hippo can therefore preach that the only way to love oneself is first to love God with one's whole self: "Love the Lord, and in so doing learn how to love yourselves, so that when by loving the Lord you genuinely love yourselves …"[11] We love ourselves by intentionally loving God and all else in and because of God; in this way self-love is always a by-product of properly ordered desires. Those who set out to love themselves directly actually end up hating themselves. That is how:

> In some inexplicable way (*inexplicabili modo*) whoever "loves" himself and not God, does not actually love himself; and whoever loves God and not himself, does in fact love himself. For the one who is not able to live from himself (*non potest uiuere de se*) perishes by loving himself—for the one who "loves" himself in such a way that he does not really live, does not actually love himself. But when God from whom this one is given life is loved, by not loving himself, he who does not love himself—precisely that he may love him from whom he has life—loves himself all the more.[12]

This proves to be one of the knottier passages of Augustine's Latin (thus the shock quotes in my translation), but clearly the term *amor* is employed equivocally throughout. As we have already seen, Augustine commits himself to the view that a person—divine, angelic, or human—necessarily loves; for all persons, then, not loving is never an option. However, what

---

[11]*s*. 90.6; Hill, *Sermons* (III/3) 452.

[12]*Jo eu. tr*. 123.5: "Nescio quo enim inexplicabili modo, quisquis seipsum, non Deum amat, non se amat; et quisquis Deum, non seipsum amat, ipse se amat. Qui enim non potest uiuere de se, moritur utique amando se: non ergo se amat, qui ne uiuat se amat. Cum uero ille diligitur de quo uiuitur, non se diligendo magis diligit, qui propterea non se diligit, ut eum diligat de quo uiuit"; CCL 36.678; my translation.

we often do is love wrongly, and this amounts to actually hating oneself. This occurs most commonly when we try to make ourselves the direct object of our love, revealing the so-called "love" we thought we had for the destruction it really is.

Often Augustine will attribute this attempt at loving ourselves directly, making ourselves the source and origin of such love, to our fascination with the wondrous creatures we are. We are right to be fascinated with the glories of the human mind and the intricacies of the human body. We are to be in awe how we straddle both heaven and earth. We should be forever amazed that God became one of us. We are right to see our exaltation in such gifts, but the moment they cease being treated as gifts and as realities we ourselves have manufactured, that exaltation becomes *peruersa*, and the creature inevitably becomes "overly pleased with himself, and he is overly pleased with himself when he defects from that immutable good which ought to please him far more than he pleases himself."[13] Why is this? At the end of his early work *On Free Choice of the Will* (*De Libero Arbitrio*), the recently ordained presbyter Augustine reflects on what true wisdom is. This is a fitting work transitioning from his earlier philosophical training into his pastoral work. For he not only wants to make sense of the *sapientia* which he strove after for so many years, he also wants to offer practical advice on how to attain it. The primal enemy of wisdom is pride, that self-centeredness which turns the created mind away from the one true Good and "folly is the consequence of turning away from wisdom" (*auersionem autem stultitia consequitur*). And why do we turn away from this sole source of blessedness?

> And whence came the turning away, if not from the fact that man, whose good God is, willed to be his own good and so to substitute himself for God. Accordingly, the Scriptures say, "Looking to myself, my soul is cast down" (Ps 42:6 LXX). And again: "Taste and ye shall be as gods" (Gen 3:5).[14]

The proud person reduces God to an aversion. For when I sense disordered affection within me, I am tempted to destroy any righteousness around me so I can cozy up more comfortably with my own sins. The ancient wisdom of Israel knew this well:

---

[13] *ciu. Dei* 14.7; Babcock, *City of God* (I/7) 119.
[14] *lib. arb.* 3.24.72; trans., John H.S. Burleigh, *Augustine: Earlier Writings* (Philadelphia: The Westminster Press, 1953) 214.

Let us lie in wait for the righteous one, because he is annoying to us; he opposes our actions, reproaches us for transgressions of the law and charges us with violations of our training. He professes to have knowledge of God and styles himself a child of the Lord. To us he is the censure of our thoughts; merely to see him is a hardship for us, because his life is not like that of others, and different are his ways. He judges us debased; he holds aloof from our paths as from things impure. He calls blest the destiny of the righteous and boasts that God is his Father. (Wis 2:12–16)

In so doing, the proud turn away from the only one who is able to satisfy their human longing for divinity. Instead we find it somehow safer to rely on our own powers. But how is this even possible? Augustine's consistent answer lies in the glorious reality of the human person.

Because the human mind in particular is so splendid, the option resides in our ability to revel in ourselves. Yet only the proud person persists in this pursuit. Augustine therefore offers an antidote to such fancy: to make a distinction (*differentia*) between Creator and the creature by distinguishing between the perfect and unchanging good for which we are made and those ephemeral, transient goods which we can enjoy but which leave us dissatisfied nonetheless. He accordingly contrasts God and the human mind:

The mind is not as God is, and yet, next to God, it can give us satisfaction. It is better when it forgets itself in love for the unchangeable God, or indeed utterly contemns itself in comparison with him. But if the mind, being immediately conscious of itself, takes pleasure in itself to the extent of perversely imitating God, wanting to enjoy its own power, the greater it wants to be the less it becomes. Pride is the beginning of all sin, and the beginning of man's pride is revolt from God.[15]

This disequilibrium between spiritual realities is a key move in the healing the divided psyche requires: as glorious the human mind is, as capable as the mind is of enjoying truth and beauty, only God can satisfy (*possit placere*). That is why the mind must allow the mutual indwelling between itself and God to occur. In Augustine's words, the soul must admit that while it is beautiful and pleasing, it is nonetheless only a creature "next to God" (*post Deum*). Divine union is the only antidote to human pride, and the

---

[15]*lib. arb.* 3.25.76; Burleigh, *Augustine*, 216.

first step in admitting this posture of creaturely humility is to recognize that apart from God, all things are to be held in contempt (*in illius comparatione contemnit*).

We have seen this sort of healthy contempt is the other side of proper self-love.[16] It is not the contempt of the self wholesale and outright, it is the contempt of that rebellious part of our souls that fights union with God. We must extinguish those desires that do not want God's indwelling, that part of us that does not want to make this necessary comparison between his greatness and our contingency. What must be slain and thus surrendered is that part of the mind where the enemy still speaks, promising divinity without the Divine, holding out godliness without God. In other words, authentic self-love means we must abandon our temptation toward a monadic, autonomous self and surrender to the loving and deifying union of the Lord. Only in allowing him to have and to hold us can the true beauty of our glorious selves be realized. Herein lies the paradox: we can only love by being loved first.

By definition, love for Augustine can never be solipsistic or self-referential. For him, this intentional turn to form an autonomous self remains the essence of the first-ever act of iniquity and the heart of all sin since. Commenting on the devil's fall, Augustine contends that a "twisted love of self deprives that swollen, puffed-up spirit of holy companions, and confines him, so eager to sate himself through wickedness in an ever hungry wretchedness."[17] Satan refused to be loved and thus loved himself wrongly. A perverse love of self turns the lover within, whereas rightly ordered charity is the realization of relationship, through which we meet love himself and through whom we are now able to love neighbor and self. Such realization begins not with our loving but with our being loved. The surrender is the sweetness and determines all else. The classical figure of this paradox, that right self-love is actually allowing another to love us first, is the handsome Hellene, Narcissus. This may seem like an unsuspected character to introduce at this stage of our study, as Augustine never mentions Narcissus, but the key movements of his story are precisely what the Bishop of Hippo is trying to work out as he explains the Christian sense of *amor sui*.

---

[16]Of course the most famous line to capture this Augustinian tenet is found at *ciu. Dei* 14.28: "Two loves have made two cities. Love of self, even to the point of contempt for God, made the earthly city, and love of God, even to the point of contempt for self, made the heavenly city," Babcock, *City of God* (I/7) 136.

[17]*Gn. Litt.* 11.15.19; Hill, *Genesis* (I/13) 439; cf. *ciu. Dei* 11.13.

The fate of Narcissus

How can one hate that which is inherently loveable? Do we first fabricate idols and then hate that fictive shadow in place of the love that would otherwise claim us as its own? As the tortured Sebastian explains to the Oxonian outsider Charles in Evelyn Waugh's classic novel: one cannot really hate God and the saints, so we instead construct an extension of their own selves and project it onto that which we are set on destroying.

> I sometimes think when people wanted to hate God they hated Mummy … You see, she was saintly, but she wasn't a saint. No one could really hate a saint, could they? They can't really hate God either. When they want to hate Him and His saints they have to find something like themselves and pretend it's God and hate that. I suppose you think that's all bosh.[18]

This is an idol for Augustine, the thing which I hate but which I also resist relinquishing. Like a moth around a flame, I know it will destroy me but I refuse to let go. By definition, an idol is manufactured and can thus be manipulated; true reality, on the other hand, determines and therefore makes demands. We have seen how Augustine's understanding of sin is a matter of loving wrongly: early on this perverse love was explained as one's preferring a lower over a higher good, while later it was more often described as a selfish sequestering of a common good only for oneself. We shall now ask how this erroneous love occurs. What happens in the psyche when one's love is actually destructive, hateful? In particular, what exactly did Augustine loathe when he loved his own ruin? How are love and hate related in his psychology of sin and desire?

As mentioned, the story of Narcissus appears nowhere in Augustine's writings, but the tale's moral on the connection between the fleeing of the other and the inevitable taking up with oneself is exactly what Augustine wants us to understand. We are made to enter into another's embrace, and that gift has to be freely accepted; but in rejecting it, one inevitably is forced to take up with him or herself, and usually in harmful ways. So, even though he does not mention Narcissus by name, students of Augustine have seen how this mythical character captures perfectly what the Bishop

---

[18]Sebastian Flyte to Charles Ryder, as in Evelyn Waugh, *Brideshead Revisited* (Boston: Little, Brown and Co., 1945) 22.

of Hippo is trying to avoid when explaining virtuous self-love. Most of us today can recall the Myth of Narcissus in fragments, aware that the flower named after this striking young man arose from his gazing too long into his own reflection. The familiar tale of Narcissus exists in various ancient editions, each with embellishments unique to different mythographer's take. So, whether it appears in classical Greek authors like Parthenius of Nicaea (d. 14 AD), or Roman authors like Ovid (d. c. 18 AD), also reemerging in William Shakespeare, John Milton, and Goethe, the kernel of the story remains basically the same. Regardless of the century and circumstance of Narcissus's appearance, he continues to stand as the archetype of self-love, self-absorption, and even maniacal egoism.

As the basic story unfolds, this beautiful young man is extraordinarily gorgeous and must suffer the lavishness and flatteries of both boys and girls throughout his youth. A dangerous mixture of conceitedness and disgust of others' fawning brews in his soul and leads him to avoid any real intimacy or any true companionship. He instead takes comfort in his own gorgeousness and physical abilities. As Ovid tells us what happened, Narcissus is out one day hunting deer alone "in the lonely countryside" (*deuia rura*—the trackless woods, emphasizing the lad's desire for solitude), when he is espied by the nymph Echo. Another eponymous figure in Greek myth, Echo has been doomed to wander repeating whatever she hears, unable ever to initiate a conversation or speak her own mind. Seeing that he has come into another's purview, Narcissus panics and flees Echo's fawning. Running he cries out, "Away with these embraces! I would die before I would have you touch me," to which she inevitably resonates, "I would have you touch me."[19] This is not simply a story about the dangers of radical self-conceit; it is a myth hoping to explain that Narcissism is the result of believing that one never need enter into communion with another. Accordingly, Narcissus outruns his pursuer and, with great satisfaction, takes up with his own face. This reflection coruscating on the water remains a symbol of Narcissus's own superficiality; unwilling to love another, he chooses to care only for himself. Infuriated by this rejection of the nymph Echo, however, the goddess of revenge Nemesis lets Narcissus grow more and more enamored with his own reflection, and he consequently becomes so fixated with his striking countenance that, paralyzed by self-love, he literally sprouts riparian roots and dies where the beautiful flower grows in his stead.

---

[19]Ovid, *Metamorphoses*, Book 3, trans., Mary Innes (New York: Penguin Classics, 1955) 84.

Turning again to the illuminating works of Paul Rigby, we see how he engaged another scholar, Donald Capps, in a series of very helpful exchanges asking if Augustine was a Narcissist. Capps argues that the *Confessions*, in particular, reveal "narcissistic personality trends (in which shame plays a major role) and a melancholy self (in which the mother–son relationship is central)." Such narcissism, Capps argues, leads Augustine to a "great deal of self-reproach" in his earlier years.[20] Capps's works focus on this intersection between a shameful self-love and the sorrow that stems from it. While Rigby agrees with much of the analysis offered by Capps, he diverges in arguing that Augustine overcame his narcissistic qualities through a committed life of ecclesial service.[21] While I personally agree with Rigby's estimation of how Augustine developed psychologically and personally, this exchange indicates how narcissism is a helpful way to approach Augustine's life story.

Keeping Narcissus in mind when we read Augustine on charity, we can better appreciate what the modern mind has forgotten about the covenanted self. Both Narcissus and Augustine teach us that without the love of another, one does not just become "selfish," one's self is utterly lost. For once Narcissus exchanges his self for an object, his life becomes depersonalized (he is transmuted into a flower) and stagnant (unable to leave the water's shore). Similarly, in Augustine's theology of charity, a person content with him or herself becomes enslaved to that false self-image. As John Cavadini has so well written:

> The content of self-awareness, for those truly self-aware, is much more disturbing and mysterious, more exciting and hopefully, more treacherous and full of risk. Someone who is self-aware is aware not of "a self" but of a struggle, a brokenness, a gift, a process of healing, a resistance to healing, an emptiness, a reference that impels one not to concentrate on oneself, in the end, but on that to which one's self-awareness propels one to God. Someone who is properly self-aware is aware of a transformation, a reconfiguring, a recreation of an identity from nothing, of a becoming better, and not of a stable entity that endures as a private inner space or object.[22]

---

[20]Donald Capps, "Augustine's Confessions: Self-Reproach and the Melancholy Self," *Pastoral Psychology* 55 (2007) 571–91; 571.

[21]Paul Rigby, "Was Augustine a Narcissist?" *Augustinian Studies* 44:1 (2013) 59–91.

[22]John Cavadini, "The Darkest Enigma: Reconsidering the Self in Augustine's Thought," *Augustinian Studies* 38 (2007) 119–32; 123.

The reflective soul sees how it is trapped between being satisfied with itself and being torn apart, all the while knowing that it can never really be enough for itself. In this fissure arises a certain self-contempt, refusing to let go of what it wrongly believes is its only security.

Unlike Narcissus whose self-contentment affixes him to the muddy shores of isolation, those who love rightly can never rest in themselves. They must always be in constant conversion, surrendering all they are and do for the sake of divine union:

> Forge ahead, my brothers and sisters; always examine yourselves without self-deception, without flattery, without buttering yourselves up. After all, there's nobody inside you before whom you need to feel ashamed, or whom you need to impress. There is someone there, but one who is pleased with what you are, if you want to arrive at what you are not yet. Because wherever you are satisfied with yourself, there you have stuck. If, though, you say, "That's enough, that's the lot," then you've even perished. Always add some more, always keep on walking, always forge ahead. Don't stop on the road, don't run round and go back, don't wander off the road. You stop, if you don't forge ahead; you go back, if you turn back to what you have already left behind; you wander off the road, if you apostatize. The lame man on the road goes better than the springer off the road.[23]

This is why we must offer ourselves entirely to the Lord as we are and not as we think he wants us. Christ the great judge lives within and he neither shames nor needs to be impressed; we are therefore instructed to make that journey of allowing Christ to receive us evermore fully without self-deception (*sine dolo*) and without any flattery (*sine adulatione*), trying to make ourselves look better than we truly are. We need not impress Christ, we need never fear of being embarrassed before him. We simply need to let him know who we truly are. And, yes, in this exchange of selves, Augustine forewarns, there is going to be some healthy dissatisfaction and maybe some embarrassment. The great convert realizes keenly that there are still sins and fallen desires that keep us from loving Christ, and being loved by him, fully. But unless our truest self is confessed and offered to the Lord, we remain imprisoned in our own false self-images—sinners unworthy of sanctity.

---

[23] *s.* 169.18; Hill, *Sermons* (III/5) 235.

But why would we choose to remain locked-in on a destructive lie? In his characteristic reading of the human psyche, Sigmund Freud saw Narcissistic Personality Disorder (NPD) as a form of self-defense, an inflation of self which disallowed anyone from committing to a truly vulnerable love. The absorbed self finds it safe to take the place where another should go, what Freud called a "libidinal investment of the self." This replacement of the other with the self precludes any opportunity for disappointment or the vulnerability necessary when one lets another into his or her own life. Freud's 1914 essay on Narcissism is well known (*Zur Einführung des Narzißmus*) and helped twentieth-century psychologists to explain many mental and social problems. Freud's work on Narcissism put this correlation between extreme autonomy and self-love into a new light. A new generation of psychologists arose after Freud, and began to realize that Freud's theories on the origins and nature of Narcissism did not fit many cases. While it is true that some patients really did have an overinflated sense of their own worth, there were just as many who suffered from a lack of self and consequently masked this emptiness with a veneer of bravado which underneath was nothing more than fear of being known and being loved.

As a Roman Catholic priest, this is a phenomenon I hear all too often in the Sacrament of Reconciliation. Many in the confessional all too casually accuse themselves of the sin of pride. It takes only a few questions, however, to help them see that they are not so much proud as they are afraid. The proud person thinks that he or she is at the center of the universe and all accomplishments are entirely his or her own. But what I actually hear from most people is an acute form of distress, a fear that is more accurately confessing something like this, "Father, I need to keep up this wall of self-sufficiency, because if my spouse or my boss or my friends ever saw how fragile I actually am inside, how little I actually know or even care, they would reject me." "I need to continue to wear this asbestos suit of self-reliance because I am afraid of entrusting myself to another." We all learn early on, however, that true love is elusive, and that relationships can be chancy. So, instead, we all learn how to hide behind the mask of self-sufficiency which very often is interpreted as pride when all along it is actually a dread of being found out.

The American Trappist monk and priest, Thomas Merton (1915–68), challenges each of us when he wrote from his cell in Gethsemane, Kentucky:

Everyone of us is shadowed by an illusory person: a false self ...
My false and private self is the one who wants to exist outside the reach of God's will and God's love—outside of reality and outside of

life. And such a self cannot help but be an illusion … All sin starts from the assumption that my false self, the self that exists only in my own egocentric desires, is the fundamental reality of life to which everything else in the universe is ordered. Thus I use up my life in the desire for pleasures and the thirst for experiences, for power, honor, knowledge, and love, to clothe this false self and construct its nothingness into something objectively real. And I wind experiences around myself and cover myself with pleasures and glory like bandages in order to make myself perceptible to myself and to the world, as I were an invisible body that could only become visible when something visible covered its surface. But there is no substance under the things with which I am clothed. I am hollow, and my structure of pleasures and ambitions has no foundation. I am objectified in them. But they are all destined by their very contingency to be destroyed. And when they are gone there will be nothing left of me but my own nakedness and emptiness and hollowness, to tell me that I am my own mistake.[24]

This is where the Narcissus story needs a new interpretation. Not all reject communion because of a puffed up sense of their own worth. It is often not an overevaluation of oneself that causes division but an unwillingness to trust in one's own desirability and worth.

Twentieth-century scholars like the psychoanalyst Heinz Kohut (1913–81) and the sociologist Richard Sennett (b. 1943) came to realize that there are two species of Narcissism. There is the type that is truly bravado, a machismo which might really insist that one is sovereign over all others. However, sitting with the pages of the *Confessions* for more than a minute or two, one quickly realizes that this is not what is plaguing our author. The young Augustine suffers deep down not from an abundance of self-love but its opposite. Here is Narcissus fleeing Echo, here is one unwilling to embrace his belovedness, unwilling to let himself matter to another. The result? Destruction. "I was in love with my own ruin." For when love is refused, only hatred remains to fill that wound. In the 1970s Kohut accordingly inaugurated a subversive reading of this cautionary tale against self-love. What Kohut began was a way of reading the Myth of Narcissus not as one about the self's inflation but rather its depletion, described by Kohut as, "subtly experienced, yet pervasive feelings of emptiness

---

[24]Thomas Merton, *New Seeds of Contemplation* (New York: New Directions Press, 1962) 34–5.

and depression."[25] According to Kohut, Narcissism is caused not by an overemphasis of one's worth but by a lack of external validation. The beautiful Narcissus enters infamy because he is unwilling to enter into relationship with Echo; he is cold and indifferent to the warmth of another. He dies *not* out of self-assuredness, but out of insecurity and an unwillingness to be received vulnerably by another.

Augustine knew this himself early on in that grove of pears and later in his tussle with the Pelagians. The Doctor of Grace came to see how sin is freely committed out of one of these two extremes: the blustery audacity of the self-assured as well as the hollowness of the depleted. After quoting Sirach's insight that "The beginning of all sin is pride" (Sir 10:15), Augustine goes on to differentiate those sins which are done out of pride and those which are done by "persons weeping and groaning." It is in the sorrow and the emptiness that we sometimes lash out and in both instances, in both the boasting as well as the weeping, we all withdraw from God which is ultimately the essence of rebellious pride.[26] This is an intriguing and illuminating reading of a self-love which results not out of bravado and self-reliance. One's turn toward oneself is the result of fearing interpersonal intimacy. Alone the self is depleted and desiccated, forced to sprout roots into its own woundedness, thereby isolating itself from any intimacy or sense of organic connectedness. Pride is still the primal sin, but now its other face is revealed. There is a form of pride that says, "Get out of my way," and another type that says, "See how insignificant I am." The former version is a pride that is full of itself and seeks to dominate over others; the latter is one that estimates itself as not worthy of another's attention and love, and so seeks to disappear. These two extremes are both manifestations of pride because both have refused to belong to a community, both insist that the rules which govern all others do not apply to them. Both groups consider themselves extraordinarily special: the first for what they think they are, the second for what they fear they are not.

In his 1979 book *The Culture of Narcissism*, the American social critic, Christopher Lasch (d. 1994), followed Kohut's insights to show how a narcissistic personality is most often manifested by these four qualities: (1) an unwillingness to be received or claimed by the other, (2) a need to

[25]Heinz Kohut, *The Analysis of the Self: A Systematic Approach to the Psychoanalytic Treatment of Narcissistic Personality Disorders* (New York: International Universities Press, 1971) 72. See too Richard Sennett's influential study, "Narcissism and Modern Culture," *October* 4 (1977) 70–9; JSTOR, www.jstor.org/stable/778482.
[26]*nat. et gr.* 29.33; Teske, *Answer to the Pelagians* (I/23) 241.

manipulate others in order to keep their impressions unspoiled, (3) an inordinately shallow emotional life, and (4) a fear of one's own finitude and personal limitations.[27] Surely we could read all four of these characteristics back into young Augustine's life's story, but what is certain is that the form of Narcissism from which Augustine suffered was not a cocky self-assuredness, but a shallow emptiness, a frustrated search. It was a form of emptiness which inevitably led to self-aggrandizement. For where we reject the transformative love of another, we must set it up for ourselves.

Narcissus's fear of intimacy closes off his heart from the givenness for which this very heart was made, deceiving him into thinking he can find himself in himself. By rejecting the other, however, Narcissus loses himself. He is transformed from man into plant, from a subject into a thing, however beautiful. This is not unlike Augustine's recalling of Alypius's loss of self in the frenzy of the gladiatorial games. Having sworn off such bloody sport, Alypius is nonetheless cajoled and dragged into the arena in Rome with his so-called friends. Confident in his own virtue, Alypius swears that, "You may drag my body into that place and fix me there, but can you direct my mind and my eyes to the show? I will be there, and yet be absent, and so get the better both of you and of the performance." But any friend of Augustine's should know how relying on one's own strength ends up in being defaced, so that he loses his own personal integrity, and thus becomes just "one of the crowd he had joined."[28] However, the entire point of the *Confessions* is that life in true Christian virtue is what allows one to have a face, a story, an identity. Vice, on the other hand, defaces and reduces one to just a member of the crowd. No longer an individual but now an object, defaced, just one more manifestation of a trust in the self that can lead only to obliteration.

This solipsistic love of self is exactly what Augustine understands as self-hatred—*odium sui* or *contemptus sui*—and the result of seeking salvation in our own selves. The created soul is made to be in intimate and deifying communion with one outside of itself; yet in its fallen need to control, it turns away and within. Augustine therefore advises:

Put no trust in yourself, but only in your God. If you trust in yourself, your soul will be turned toward yourself and gravely troubled, because

---

[27]Christopher Lasch, *The Culture of Narcissism: American Life in an Age of Diminishing Expectations* (New York: Warner Books, 1979) 75–87. For a more spiritual reading of this tale, Louis Lavelle, *The Dilemma of Narcissus* (London: George Allen & Unwin Ltd, 1973).
[28]*conf.* 6.8.13; Boulding, *Confessions* (I/1) 146.

it cannot yet find any grounds for security in you. So, then, if my soul turned toward myself and found itself disturbed, what is left to me but humility, the humble refusal of the soul to place any reliance on itself?[29]

For Augustine, then, to avoid self-destruction means to love oneself rightly. Sadly, the fallen soul finds immediate comfort in misplaced loves and considers that self-care: "if you love iniquity, can you pretend to love yourself?"[30] But what is this iniquity? Ultimately, it is the inversion when I consider myself as the source of love and not first its recipient.

Charity for Augustine first demands my allowing God to love me, and then only in that reception am I able love myself rightly and all others whom God himself loves. This is the only way I can avoid destroying myself: by recognizing and surrendering to the only origin and source of all my loves, Love himself. If I refuse to acknowledge God here, I inevitably set up another which is not God in his place. Bad theology is nothing other than idolatry. Augustine comes to see how and why he must dethrone any false images of God if he is ever going to shun the sorrow he has come to recognize in loving wrongly: "for wheresoever a human soul turns, it can but cling to what brings sorrow unless it turns toward you."[31] Our focus now can treat this alliance between false loving and idols in Augustine's theology of charity, coming to see how misplaced self-love leads ultimately to self-destruction.

The paradox of idolatrous loves

Of all the popes the Catholic Church has seen, the most Augustinian in tone and in theology is arguably Pope Emeritus Benedict XVI, Joseph Ratzinger (b. 1927). As a young theologian, Ratzinger wrote a dissertation on Augustine's ecclesiology and another on "the medieval Augustine," St. Bonaventure and his theology of history. While these sorts of things are rarely disclosed to the public, perhaps the last thing Benedict wrote as reigning pope was some part or parts of the 2013 papal encyclical *Lumen Fidei*, which according to Benedict's successor Pope Francis, was admittedly

---

[29]*en. Ps.* 41.12; Boulding, *Expositions* (III/16) 250.
[30]*en. Ps.* 140.2; Boulding, *Expositions* (III/20) 302.
[31]*conf.* 4.10.15; Boulding, *Confessions* (I/1) 101.

a writing of "four hands." It should come as no surprise, then, to find essentially Augustinian insights throughout. So, while we may never know Pope Emeritus Benedict's direct involvement in the writing of *Lumen Fidei*, it is nevertheless significant that Pope Francis chose to open his pontificate with an encyclical on the power of the Christian faith to unite one's life story around a God whose love gathers the faithful and saves them from following the idols fabricated from their own deficiencies. One can choose to live this life either in union with a loving God who serves as both path and purpose, or in the disintegration of having no ultimate end and, therefore, no true journey but only uncollected moments of experiences, however thrilling, which fail to bring any satisfaction whatsoever. This latter way of life Francis calls polytheism in that the self-divinization of creatures can never make one happy, for such false deities must always be destroyed and continuously replaced:

> Once man has lost the fundamental orientation which unifies his existence, he breaks down into the multiplicity of his desires; in refusing to await the time of promise, his life-story disintegrates into a myriad of unconnected instants. Idolatry, then, is always polytheism, an aimless passing from one lord to another. Idolatry does not offer a journey but rather a plethora of paths leading nowhere and forming a vast labyrinth. Those who choose not to put their trust in God must hear the din of countless idols crying out: "Put your trust in me!" Faith, tied as it is to conversion, is the opposite of idolatry; it breaks with idols to turn to the living God in a personal encounter. Believing means entrusting oneself to a merciful love which always accepts and pardons, which sustains and directs our lives, and which shows its power by its ability to make straight the crooked lines of our history. Faith consists in the willingness to let ourselves be constantly transformed and renewed by God's call. Herein lies the paradox: by constantly turning towards the Lord, we discover a sure path which liberates us from the dissolution imposed upon us by idols.[32]

This is *so Augustinian*, a perfect summary of the early books of the *Confessions*. Here is a most mysterious aspect of sin—the isolating hatred and sabotaging of oneself. Why would anyone prefer his or her own self-

---

[32]Pope Francis, *Lumen Fidei* §13 (Washington, DC: United States Conference of Catholic Bishops, 2013) 10.

imposed brokenness over another's promise of healing? As Pope Francis asks: Why do we whimsically chase idols without purpose rather than entrust ourselves wholeheartedly to a love that promises not to fail? Reading Augustine we begin to see that his understanding of things just might hold an answer to these perplexing questions. Relationships can be precarious and oftentimes ambiguous; opening ourselves up to receive and thus depend on another is too humbling. It is far less demanding to keep myself at the center of reality and thereby refuse to submit to the demands of another. But we tear at ourselves when we sense these idols within us. In our incessant restlessness, we erect our own idols out of our illusory need to control; in our incessant restlessness, we then tear them down knowing they will never bring the true rest we seek.

In his self-loathing, Augustine has not yet learned that love is audaciously greater than imperfection. Out of a certain type of misplaced piety, he safely disentangles reality into two stories: "people would rather hold that you suffer evil than that we commit it."[33] As such, there can be no cohesion, no unity, no one narrative, and thus no salvation. Augustine is unwilling to let God be present in his brokenness and divided interiority; he is unwilling to admit that the divine longs to enter the darkness. Augustine therefore searches out a deity who is alienated from all that is, a god of reproach and resentment. He has not yet come to the embodiment and the passion of a God who becomes sin out of love for others (cf. 1 Cor 5:21). The younger Augustine's response therefore is to mimic the Manichean dualism by setting up another divine corollary which, only later, is he able to see how it was "a temple for its own idol and an abomination."[34] In these early years he still resists unveiling the God of the Catholic creeds, refusing to allow love to claim him as he is in all his brokenness and fear. That is, he holds on to his melancholy and the bitter gall of self-loathing that has built up in his soul. He will not relinquish control of all that which he believed could not be received by the one good God, and thus sequesters and sets up an idolatrous place of worship within his own heart. Here he becomes divided: divided between a God whom he dare not admit is anything other than purity, unable to admit the imperfect into its presence, and an evil extension of his own fallenness which he forces to receive only disobedience and decay.

When we debase and so replace God, we inevitably debase and divide ourselves as well: "you yourself worship what you deprecate being, and by

---

[33] conf. 7.3.5; Boulding, *Confessions* (I/1) 166.
[34] conf. 7.14.20; Boulding, *Confessions* (I/1) 175–6.

worshipping it you are to a certain extent turned into something like it. Not so that you become a piece of wood and cease to be a human being, but since you make your inner self into something like what you have made outwardly."[35] When we become alienated from the source of our desires, we became alienated against ourselves, dehumanized, ending in sorrow and malice. Understanding sinfulness in this way was an important move in Augustine's extradition out of Manichaeism. An intelligible cosmos demands a single locus of divinity but the dualist is forever divided. Before Augustine came to see evil not as a separate and active entity but as a matter of the fallen will, he was unable to accept how imperfect existents could still enjoy a place in the kingdom of the all-good God:

> There is no wholesomeness (*sanitas*) for those who find fault with anything you have created, as there was none for me when many of the things you have made displeased me. Since my soul did not dare to find my God displeasing, it was unwilling to admit that anything that displeased it was truly yours. This was why it had strayed away into believing in a duality of substances, but there it found no rest, and only mouthed the opinions of others. Turning back again it had made for itself a god extended through infinite space, all-pervasive, and had thought this god was you, and had set him up in its heart; so it became yet again a temple for its own idol and an abomination in your sight.[36]

Having finally cast off the tenets of Manichaeism, he came to see sin no longer as the battle between two distinct camps, but as a civil war with wayward children trying to run away from their ever-loving Father. All things are metaphysically good and there is no-thing that is not desired, created and sustained by a devoted, omnipotent God. All is his. The idols and the "abominations in God's sight" that we create are fashioned when we are unwilling to allow this God to be the Lord of *all* of our lives, the Lord of every aspect and experience.

There is an amazing section in the *Catechism of the Catholic Church* which captures this inevitability of idolization of the Divine if one cannot understand the love of Christ. Almost 1,500 years after the *Confessions*, this psychologically rich paragraph captures much of what Augustine was out to teach us. This particular section has to do with praying the *Our Father* and

---

[35]*s.* 23B; Hill, *Sermons* (III/11) 39.
[36]*conf.* 7.14.20; Boulding, *Confessions* (I/1) 175–6.

realizing that it is the Christ who gains for us the true understanding of God and not merely an estimate of our own fallen experiences:

> Before we make our own this first exclamation of the Lord's Prayer [*Our Father* ...], we must humbly cleanse our hearts of certain false images drawn "from this world." Humility makes us recognize that "no one knows the Son except the Father, and no one knows the Father except the Son and anyone to whom the Son chooses to reveal him," that is, "to little children" (Mt 11:25–7). The purification of our hearts has to do with paternal or maternal images, stemming from our personal and cultural history, and influencing our relationship with God. God our Father transcends the categories of the created world. To impose our own ideas in this area "upon him" would be to fabricate idols to adore or pull down. To pray to the Father is to enter into his mystery as he is and as the Son has revealed him to us.[37]

To pray truly is to understand rightly. The God of Jesus Christ is not what the world or the Manicheans or the Neoplatonists say he is. As Augustine came to learn, this is the God of Triune Love, and even he himself admits that his journey was fraught with continual realizations that what he thought was true was in fact an erroneous image. He came to see that he hated a characterization of the Catholic faith but not the actual realities thereof.[38]

What is especially intriguing about this passage from the *Catechism* is the connection between faulty theological imagery and idolatry. Collecting our past experiences, we tend to project our earthly images and experiences upon God. This of course is the reverse of what we should do as Jesus's brothers and sisters, as "every family in heaven and on earth is named" from the Father and not vice versa (Eph 3:15). If we affix our faulty images of love upon God, we shall never know the power of divine mercy and union. We shall never know ourselves. If we do not allow the fullness of God's self, a self that is so in love with fallen humanity that he is ready to die and atone for our sins, we have an ersatz deity that we can only worship wrongly from afar or tear down and trample into pieces. Wholesomeness, *sanitas*, comes only when we understand that God is a God of love and that no existent

---

[37]*Catechism of the Catholic Church* §2779.

[38]*conf.* 5.10.20: "When my mind attempted to speed back once more to the Catholic faith I was repelled, because the Catholic faith is not what I thought it was"; Boulding, *Confessions* (I/1) 128; "Against this background, however, I now began to prefer Catholic doctrine." *conf.* 6.5.7; Boulding, *Confessions* (I/1) 137.

falls outside of his charity and care. If one thinks oneself unworthy of such unconditional acceptance, as I maintain Augustine did on the evening of the great pear robbery, one cannot help but think of something which must now be torn down, a being unworthy of acceptance and forgiveness; the exact sort of person that must be destroyed.

In a sermon dated 420 and believed to have been delivered in the Basilica of the Ancestors (one of the major worship spaces in Carthage), Augustine makes this link between false self-love and idolatry explicit. His theme is the reciprocal nature of love and the theme that we have been exploring in this chapter: proper self-love, as he constantly exhorts his congregants to love God with God (*amemus Deum de Deo*). They must therefore understand that the truest loves in their lives must be distinguished from the fabricated feelings that can very easily masquerade as charity. The truth is that we can love rightly only with the love who is God. We love God with and from God, we love neighbor only when it is God who binds us together. Because love is the Holy Spirit, there is no natural or merely human love for Augustine. We shall return to this when we treat the Incarnation in the next chapter and concentrate on the Christ who alone makes love of God and love of human neighbor inseparable. But now let us take up this connection between an improper love of self and idolatry by turning to Augustine's sermon 34 where he provides a succinct theology of charity and the true love of self.

This crucial and unavoidable desire for self-love can be fulfilled only in the one in whose image and likeness each of us is made. As we have been tracing, all human persons love, but Augustine is intent on having us see that the only love that will last eternally is received from God's own self. To experience this new reality, created persons must first respond to God's initiative and thereby receive the love he is:

> There is no one of course who doesn't love, but the question is, what do they love? So we are not urged not to love, but choose what we love. But what choice can we make unless we are first chosen, since we cannot even love unless we are first loved? ... We ourselves have loved. And where did we get this from? *Because he has first loved us.* Inquire where a person gets the ability to love God from, and absolutely the only discovery you will make is that it is because God has first loved him. He has given us himself, the one we have loved; he has given us what to love with.[39]

---

[39] *s.* 34.2; Hill, *Sermons* (III/2) 166.

The only way to love in Augustine's view is first to surrender to God. Therein one enjoys the mutual indwelling of love, of the Holy Spirit's very presence, not only in the individual soul but in the right relations between other persons as well.

As the Holy Spirit thus conjoins not only an individual to God but to each of his or her neighbors as well, Augustine worries that the glories of the created order, being so marvelous in capacity and ability, possess an unnatural proclivity to substitute themselves for God as the determiner of reality. We do this most often when we consider our mind and its ability to imagine the *fons et origo* of charity, mistaking itself for the one true God:

> So why does human imagination with its flight of fancy fashion God for itself and manufacture an idol in the mind, composing it as best its thoughts may, and not as its objective search ought? "Is God like this? No, he's like that." Why sketch an outline, why arrange limbs, why provide him with an unacceptable stature, why imagine a beautiful body? *God is love.* What color has love, what outline, what shape? We see none of these things in it, and yet we love.[40]

Idolatry occurs when we confuse the true love who is the Trinity, and the true love which can come only from God, with the natural affection creatures naturally have for those whom they find attractive. Augustine therefore transitions into an examination of the affections. He has us next consider a man who falls in love (so he thinks) with a beautiful woman, but hearing that she despises him, begins to hate and ridicule the very body which initially allured him: "If he hears that she hates him, doesn't all that hot, urgent passion roused by her beautiful figure grow cold … doesn't he even begin to hate what he had previously loved?." We end up hating what we do not love rightly, and since many of his parishioners have surely experienced such attraction and subsequent repulsion, Bishop Augustine asks his people to see what it is they are really attracted to—not physical voluptuousness, but loving and being loved in return: "And yet love is loved, though it is not seen."[41] In this way, he tries to raise our understanding of what love really is, not the biological move to that which the senses find pleasing, but God's gift of self. The alternative is to try to love autonomously, imagining ourselves as the source of charity. But we are told over and over that, "You

---

[40]*s.* 34.3; Hill, *Sermons* (III/2) 167.
[41]*s.* 34.4; Hill, *Sermons* (III/2) 167.

love yourself only because you love God with your whole self" (*Ex hoc diligis te, quia Deum diligis ex toto te*).[42] We again learn how alone the self is not only sterile but destructive. When we love another or ourselves wrongly, we shall inevitably tear them down, like an idol which mocks our shortcomings that we rush to extinguish.

Destroying what we have hurt is constant. Recall, for instance, Harper Lee's classic *To Kill a Mockingbird*, and Atticus Finch's concluding statements in the pivotal courtroom scene. With Mayella on trial, Atticus admits he has nothing but sorrow for this white girl who both coquettishly attempted to seduce the black Tom Robinson, and also ruthlessly sought to destroy him. Atticus explains why:

> She is the victim of cruel poverty and ignorance, but I cannot pity her; she is white. She knew full well the enormity of her offense, but because her desires were stronger than the code she was breaking, she persisted in breaking it. She persisted, as her subsequent reaction is something that all of us have known at one time or another. She did something every child has done—she tried to put the evidence of her offense away from her. But in this case she was no child hiding stolen contraband: she struck out at her victim—of necessity she must put him away from her—he must be removed from her presence, from this world. She must destroy the evidence of her offense.[43]

Like Augustine and his attraction to the pears, a sort of suitor rejected by the beauty he thought would fulfill, Mayella Ewell is in love with the object of her own ruin as well. A white girl in 1930s Alabama, Mayella flirts with her object of desire seemingly because he is forbidden. Forced to face her divided psyche once in the public eye, she has to turn the object of her desire into the object of her destruction. She must tear down the good that reminds her of her evil, tear apart the beauty that reveals her own ugliness.

Seductive and idolatrous, a fictional reality woos false lovers inward. They turn from God and neighbor, rejecting the very origin of their ability to reject, hating the very one who alone can keep them from hating. Is this not the opening line documented in every domestic abuse file? Isolation before destruction: the abuser first controls and cuts off the abused, isolating her from her friends and family, her passions and heart's desires. The abuser

---

[42]*s.* 34.8; Hill, *Sermons* (III/2) 169.
[43]Harper Lee, *To Kill a Mockingbird* (New York: Harper Perennial [1960] 2002) 231, chapter 20.

alleges that he alone should be enough, that only he understands her and can thereby determine the reality in which she will now live. He must isolate before he can strike. He manipulates and separates, and then denigrates and demolishes. "Why aren't I enough for you?" "Why is that friend, your work, or that hobby so important to you?"

Psychic isolation always leads to ontological destruction. Seeing this helped me to understand why the internal alienation of the self which Augustine works out at *Trin.* 12 leads to questions of self-love and ruin in Book 14:

> So the man who knows how to love himself loves God; and the man who does not love God, even though he loves himself, which is innate in him by nature, can still be said quite reasonably to hate himself when he does what is against his own interest, and stalks himself as if he were his own enemy. It is indeed a dreadful derangement that while everyone wants to do himself good, many people do nothing but what is absolutely destructive of themselves. The poet describes a disease of this sort that afflicts dumb animals:
>
> Ye gods, for pious men a better lot,/ this wild derangement for your foes preserve!/Their own limbs with unsheathed teeth they tore.[44]

When we are covered in sin, we become blind to our own ruin. In loving wrongly, we destroy ourselves with our own "unsheathed teeth." And why do we do it? When I turn away from beauty, I can feel better about my own foulness; when I reject the good in and around me, my own evil can go unchallenged. In its embrace, love shines a redeeming light upon the beloved and if I cannot stand it, I must extinguish that light of love—"And this is the verdict, that the light came into the world, but people preferred darkness to light, because their works were evil" (Jn 3:19).

Preferring tenebrous evil to the freeing light is the paradox of sin for Augustine. It is a form of self-sabotage that springs from the fallen soul's desire to disappear, to refuse communion. As a result, the evils we find comforting are nothing more than idols who consume us:

> What you love is iniquity, your most implacable enemy, who doesn't attack you from without, but is foisted upon you by yourself from within. To help it defeat you all the more easily, you are more biased

---

[44]*Trin.* 14.18; Hill, *The Trinity* (I/5) 384–5; citing Virgil, *Georgics* 3.513.

in its favor against yourself. Thus you are plainly convicted of hating yourself, since you love that by which you are shamefully defeated. Indeed, the divine utterance could hardly be mistaken which declares, *But whoever loves iniquity hates his own soul.* (Ps 11:5)[45]

Augustine situates his analysis of self-destruction here in a larger question of proper self-love. We are free to hate ourselves but we do so by trying to love ourselves in improper ways. Those who love themselves wrongly actually hate themselves and hence with unsheathed teeth rip themselves apart. In short, the hurt hurts: "Brothers and sisters, I'll say it to you more bluntly, and as far as the Lord grants me, freely: It's only bad people who vent their rage on bad people."[46] Those who rage against themselves inevitably lash out at those around them, but perhaps even worse, this ripping and tearing does not stop with our neighbor but even burrows into our very selves. As Augustine preached, Christ is good to us when we are bad and even more tender when, "We are savage (*saiuientes*) against our selves."[47]

Therefore, the only solution to this self-loathing and destruction is the acceptance of love. This is why Love came into the world, or as Augustine seems to sum up the Church's entire theology on why the Son of God became human: "Thus, before all else, Christ came so that people might learn how much God loves them, and might learn this so that they would catch fire with love for him who first loved them."[48] To overcome this attachment to our destructive self, Augustine would advise us to do two things: first, recognize that only union with God is going to satiate and satisfy our deepest longings; and, second, see how union with God can now be approached only through the humanity of Christ Jesus—the Way leading to God the Father. The Augustinian approach is never, therefore, a "God-and-me" solitary affair, and it is never a spirituality that is going to insist on "God alone." To deny oneself is to live no longer as a self but as a "we." As Augustine sees things, to be wholly fulfilled, a human person must live always and everywhere relationally, nuptially, as a member of the Body of Christ, as a temple in whom the Holy Spirit personally dwells. It is to this invitation to eternal union that we now turn.

---

[45]*s.* 35.2; Hill, *Sermons* (III/2) 172.

[46]*s.* 302.16; Hill, *Sermons* (III/8) 308.

[47]*s.* 29A.2; Hill, *Sermons* (III/2) 121; this same phrased is used at *s.* 359.7 when Bishop Augustine exhorts his flock to be patient with (and even to become a nuisance to) those who rage against the Church, as only mercy can soften and win over the hurting heart.

[48]*cat. rud.* 1.4.8; Canning, *Instructing Beginners in the Faith* (I/10) 70.

Conclusion

We love ourselves rightly only when we allow God to love us first. In so doing, we overcome Augustine's early Manichean fears and allow love to draw near to imperfection, allow love to approach and mend our divided hearts.

> Long for Christ's friendship and you will be safe. He wants to be your guest. Make a place for him. What do I mean by telling you to make a place for him? Do not love yourself, but love him. If you are in love with yourself, you shut the door in his face; but if you are in love with him, you open it to him. If you open it and he comes in, you will no longer be in danger of being lost through self-love; when he loves you, you will be found.[49]

In loving Christ first, we receive the only love with which we can love ourselves and our neighbor. Opening to him, surrendering to him, allowing him into our hearts are the ways Augustine expresses this moment of capitulation.

Without admitting Love into our souls, idols inevitably arise therein. Like Narcissus, if we refuse extrapersonal communion, we are left with no one but our selves. But our selves are created to run on community. We are created to find ourselves in the renunciation of an autonomous self in exchange for a covenanted, communal self. Perhaps we today live in the age of the "selfie," because we have turned away so subtly from the one, true living God in exchange for a world of ephemerality and sheen that we have created only for ourselves. Perhaps we now live in the age of the "selfie," because we have no one truly next to us who could capture our life's story. Idolatry of this kind is the result of refusing communion, and Augustine spends his life teaching that only a God-made human can save humans from trying to become their own gods.

---

[49]*en. Ps.* 131.6; Boulding, *Expositions* (III/20) 159–60.

CHAPTER 5
ATONEMENT AND THE VULNERABLE CHRIST

> How else but through a broken heart
> May Lord Christ enter in?[1]

So far in our study we have followed those made to become like God through a series of choices undertaken so as to fulfill that innate invitation. As creatures constituted to love, human persons must come to discover what proper love is, and what the true origin and goal of all loving is. Most of our lives are instances of stops and starts in this regard, often learning what true charity is only after heartbreak and disappointment. But as we hopefully mature and grow in grace, we come to see how the Triune God is the only one able to complete those made in his image and likeness, and that to love oneself rightly is to open oneself to God's pattern of interpersonal union first and foremost:

> The more God's charity is sovereign in a person, the less dominion does iniquity have over him. If this is so, what is the psalmist asking in the present verse [viz., Ps 118:133], if not that by God's gift he may love God? By loving God he also loves himself, so that he may love his neighbor as himself with the love that leads to salvation. And on these two precepts the whole law and the prophets depend. What else does the psalmist's prayer amount to but a petition that the commandments God imposes by his authority he may cause to be fulfilled by his aid?[2]

According to Augustine, this commandment to love God and neighbor became possible only once God became our neighbor. The Incarnation of the Father's only begotten Son marks the new age for Augustine because it

---

[1]Oscar Wilde, "The Ballad of Reading Gaol," 617–18, *Complete Poetry* (Oxford: Oxford University Press, 2009) 171.
[2]*en. Ps.* 118, *exp.*27.6; Boulding, *Expositions* (III/19) 474.

ushers in a new way of loving. In this way, the Incarnation did not end in Bethlehem but is ongoing as Christ's faithful surrender themselves to his atoning love, reconciling both neighbors and nations, but also mending the divided heart that plagues everyone far from God.

The divine's becoming human is therefore the supreme and unsurpassable gift of self. By the Son of God's emptying himself, he creates the space in which all men and women from all time are regathered into one. He lives for creatures, he dies for sinners. Only here does God become my neighbor, only here am I one with all of humanity. For Augustine, the Christ—God made flesh—is always a "we" in that the "whole Christ" (or in Augustine's Latin, *Christus totus*) has become all that we are, and in so doing, invites us to become all that he is. This is the Savior who plays the star role in Augustine's theology: not so much the Jesus who walked the dusty roads of Palestine, but the Christ who "labors in you, and thirsts in you, and hungers in you, and endures tribulations in you. He is still dying in you, as you have already risen in him."[3] Or as we hear most often, his love for the poor and persecuted is especially where our God now lives, because "Christ himself is the poor man."[4] Augustine was enough of a Churchman to realize that God's breaking into human history was the singular deciding factor of all human fate, but he was also enough of a mystic to see how the Incarnation is still ongoing as Christ the Head is continuously building up his Body on earth, seeking to dwell and deify every human soul who allows him a home.

This reconciliation is Augustine's sense of atonement. While any theory of atonement could not be responsibly handled in a chapter, we shall proceed by focusing on three main areas of Augustine's theology of salvation which will bring greater light to his understanding of sin as self-loathing, and will bring to a close how Jesus Christ is for him the only remedy to a heart that wants to keep itself at the center of all that supposedly is. The first section, then, will take up Augustine's insistence that we must find ourselves "displeasing." Here he counsels that what must be denied in following Christ isn't the truest self, but that self which iniquitously wants to be its own sovereign. The second section will treat Augustine's theology of atonement. As mentioned, fuller and much more comprehensive works are needed (and do in fact exist) to handle all the intricacies and central points of any great Christian's understanding of how God reconciles sinners to himself, but we shall look at three major steps in Augustine. The first is how the New Adam

---

[3] *en. Ps.* 100.3; Boulding, *Expositions* (III/19) 33.
[4] *en. Ps.* 39.28; Boulding, *Expositions* (III/16) 221.

is able to empty himself in such a way that he now identifies with every human who ever lived; the second step is how this new Lord incorporates into himself these needy creatures into his own body; while the third step is the transformation of sinner into saint or, as boldly as Augustine himself will put it, Christians into Christ. The consequence of this transformation is the third and final section of this concluding chapter, the unification of loves in Jesus Christ. Augustine is simply brilliant in discussing how if God is love, love is God, and we no longer need to fear that our true and proper love of neighbor must be in competition with our love of God.

Vulnerable and deformity: The call to find oneself displeasing

Placing another at the center of our lives means relinquishing control and thus allowing ourselves to be vulnerable—able to be wounded. Reflecting on Augustine's reaction to the loss of his friend back in *conf.* 4, C.S. Lewis saw how Augustine early on tried to love without cost and without the dangers and difficulties of openness before another. And, as only Lewis can do, he put Love's willingness to be wounded into a most memorable idiom: *to love at all is to be vulnerable*:

There is no escape along the lines St. Augustine suggests. Nor along any other lines. There is no safe investment. To love at all is to be vulnerable. Love anything, and your heart will certainly be wrung and possibly broken. If you want to make sure of keeping it intact, you must give your heart to no one, not even to an animal. Wrap it carefully round with hobbies and little luxuries; avoid all entanglements; lock it up safe in the casket or coffin of your selfishness. But in that casket— safe, dark, motionless, airless—it will change. It will not be broken; it will become unbreakable, impenetrable, irredeemable. The alternative to tragedy, or at least to the risk of tragedy, is damnation. The only place outside of Heaven where you can be perfectly safe from all the dangers and perturbations of love is Hell.[5]

This "ability to be wounded" is the Christian tradition's answer to our escaping the fate of Narcissus and the sinful (but safe) instinct to repel relationality by isolating ourselves. To love is to open ourselves up to another, to allow

[5]C.S. Lewis, *The Four Loves* (New York: Harcourt Brace [1960] 1988) 121.

another set of eyes to take notice of who we are and how we are filling our days. Charity consists in seeing myself in what is not myself but in time and through love gradually becomes me. This kind of vulnerability means we allow ourselves to be brought to places we probably do not want to go on our own. It means finding our hearts beating in the lives of another, the first step in other-centered openness that we might not otherwise take if all reality were up to us. However, in a faint imitation of the wholly heterotelic persons of the Divine Trinity, it entails (in a creaturely manner) to grow not more self-reliant and strong but more available and reliant before the other.

So how do we reach this goal? Augustine's answer seems at first to be pastorally quite unsensitive: to find ourselves displeasing. We must learn to detect any part of our souls that refuses to be vulnerable before another. "Find no pleasure in yourself (*Displice tibi*), and let him be your delight who made you; because what you find displeasing in yourself is what you have yourself brought about in you."[6] What does he mean by telling his flock to find themselves displeasing? Where is the love of Christ and the need to know that we are God's eternal beloved? Remember, Augustine is preaching out of a Tradition that tells us to deny ourselves (Mt 16:24) and to hate our very lives (Jn 12:25). How does he handle such seemingly contrary commands to God's passionate care for his creatures?

Like self-love, Augustine's comments on self-denial are paradoxical and powerful. He teaches his flock that they are of course to follow Jesus's injunction to deny themselves, but not because they themselves are bad and in need of existential eradication. Quite the opposite: to deny ourselves in an Augustinian sense is in fact to make ourselves more vulnerably communal. To deny our*selves* means to find *ourselves* in the other, to lose ourselves in Jesus Christ by allowing him to be our life's leader and light:

> "Let him deny himself, if he loves himself." By loving himself, you see, he loses himself; by denying himself, he finds himself. *Whoever loves his soul*, he says, *let him lose it* (Jn 12:25) ... *Whoever loves, let him lose.* It is a painful thing to lose what you love. But from time to time, even the farmer loses what he sows. He brings it out, scatters it, throws it away, buries it ... So that's the meaning of "Let him deny himself"; let him not lose himself by crookedly loving himself (*ne peruerse eam amando perdat se*).[7]

---

[6] *en. Ps.* 44.9; Boulding, *Expositions* (III/16) 289.
[7] *s.* 330.2; Hill, *Sermons* (III/9) 186.

The danger in such language is the thinking that to deny oneself in order to follow Jesus more closely entails the destruction of myself. This is an error many in the Christian tradition have made but it is one far from which Augustine stays. What needs to be hated and denied for Augustine is not the self that longs for communion, but that fallen part of the soul that runs away and denies its need for interpersonal union. It is the Narcissus in all of us, that part that actually believes the enemy's lie that we can be god without God, beautiful without Beauty. This is what our author finds displeasing and, quite frankly, ugly.

Commenting on Ps 103[104]:1, that *the Lord has clothed himself with majesty and splendor,* Augustine contrasts God's beauty with our ugliness. In rather erotic language, he preaches how in our isolation we are really craving to be noticed, embraced, and even kissed. Christ the bridegroom therefore has "bedewed his lips" (Ps 45:2) and waits for us to offer ourselves to him. But focusing on our sinfulness impedes our freedom to enter into this relationship; we all sense deep down that we are unworthy of such love, and so choose to stay isolated in our ugliness. This impasse however is broken by the Incarnation where God robes himself in our broken humanity and so, Augustine asks:

> Do you want to please him? You cannot please him as long as you are ugly, but what will you do to become beautiful? First of all, you must find your deformity displeasing, and then you will receive beauty from him whom you hope to please by being beautiful. He who formed you in the beginning will reform you ... If in your ugly condition you find yourself repulsive, you are already pleasing to your beautiful bridegroom ... What are you to do? Since your ugliness is offensive even to yourself, your first step must be to approach him by confession ... Begin by admitting your ugliness, the deformity of soul that results from sins and iniquity. Initiate your confession by accusing yourself of this ugliness, for as you confess you become more seemly. And who grants this to you? Who else but he who is fairer than any of humankind?[8]

Admitting our ugliness is tantamount to saying that there is something in me that does not want to belong to Christ. This is what Augustine means by denying oneself. To make ourselves vulnerable is to deny that part of our

---

[8] *en. Ps.* 103, *exp.* 1.4; Boulding, *Expositions* (III/19) 110–11.

self that refuses to be tender and other-centered. It means to crucify the self which fights against communion and the possibility of being embraced by another. It is that sniggling part of ourselves that seems to enjoy punishing ourselves with harmful habits, demeaning images, and lies about ourselves. It is that part of our fallen souls which makes "being in love with our own ruin" even possible.

The beginning of atonement is vulnerability because only by admitting our woundedness do we make room for God to heal us. Even that confession of sin is ultimately God's tender presence within those humbled enough to cry out to him:

> The one who confesses his sins and accuses himself of his sins, does it together with God. God accuses your sins; if you also accuse yourself, you join yourself to God. There are, so to say, two things: a human being and a sinner. You hear "human being," God made that being. You hear "sinner," the human being made the sinner. Eliminate what you have made, so that God may save what he has made.[9]

In his goodness, God has made us human; in our sin, we have made ourselves less than human. The double-mindedness of every sinner is what must first be discerned and then the (false) self that is the sinner must be denied, while the (true) self that is God's must be nurtured.

Where followers of Jesus usually fail is in admitting that offering him our ugliness and sinfulness is actually the initial act of praise. Augustine therefore instructs his people to locate their brokenness and admit that it is still part of who they are. In discerning and naming their imperfections, the Bishop of Hippo consoles his flock; they are not disappointing the Lord but actually allowing him to be the Savior of their lives:

> You are not being told, "Be something less than you are," but "Understand what you are. Understand that you're weak, understand that you are merely human, understand that you are a sinner. Understand that he is the one who justifies, understand that you are defiled." Let the defilement of your heart reveal itself in your confession, and you will belong to Christ's flock. Because the confession of sins is for sure an invitation to the doctor to come and cure, just as the one who in

---

[9]*Jo. eu. tr.* 12.13; Hill, *Homilies on the Gospel of John* (I/12) 239–40; for more instances of this distinction, *c. Jul.* 4.28, *en. Ps.* 140.14.

his sickness says, "I am perfectly well, thank you," is not seeking the services of the doctor.[10]

It is not to sinners Jesus has harsh and challenging words. It is to the Pharisee whose self-righteous deceives him into a sort of self-righteousness, a judging of others because he thinks he is perfectly well. Accordingly, when Augustine instructs a Christian to deny him or herself, then, he does not mean to destroy oneself as has been sometimes lived out in Christ's members; for if we are to follow the Lord's many injunctions to deny ourselves, we must first and always have a self to deny. That is, whereas Augustine's call to deny oneself involves the graced discernment of knowing what false self still resists Christ.

To do otherwise is to subscribe to, what Eleonore Stump has labeled, a "stern minded Christianity."[11] In her groundbreaking work on theodicy, *Wandering in Darkness*, Stump illustrates her concept of stern-mindedness with tales of saints who have interpreted Christ's call for his disciples to deny themselves as an invitation to obliterate themselves. But, as she makes clear, Christianity is clearly not an extreme form of Buddhism that sees the basic problem of evil as the unique desires and unrepeatable individuality of each and every human person. Stump draws from an infamous story found in John Cassian (d. 435) who is touted as the Father of Western monasticism, and invoked as a saint in the Eastern Church. Cassian relates this story with wonderful satisfaction: a man eponymously named Patermutus (the silent father) longs to enter a desert monastery after the death of his wife. He therefore seeks admittance into the most renowned monastery deep in the Egyptian Thebaid. Abba John grants Patermutus and his eight-year-old son admittance on one condition, the silent father must prove his obedience and desire to live for Christ alone. So, in full view of all the brothers, Abba John commences to slap the boy, to berate him, and show him all sorts of insults. True to his name, Patermutus says nothing and remains, Cassian tells us, "unmoved" by the boy's cheeks "streaking with the dry traces of tears." We are even told that such chilliness was achieved "out of Patermutus's love for Christ." Having survived this first round of trials, Abbot John instructs

---

[10]*s*. 137.4; Hill, *Sermons* (III/4) 374.
[11]Eleonore Stump, *Wandering in Darkness* (Oxford: Oxford University Press, 2010); in these pages, Stump coins the term "stern-minded Christianity" to describe a type of Christian denial of self that sees the problem not as double-mindedness but as the very self which must be nullified in order to be consecrated.

Patermutus to hurl his son off the monastery walls into the Nile River below, and he warmly accepts this command "as if he had been ordered to do so by the Lord," hurling the boy headlong. Of course there are monks positioned along the river to snatch the boy safely, but such hagiography even ends with Cassian's telling us that all of this was done because Patermutus's "faith and devotion were so acceptable to God that they were immediately confirmed by divine testimony."[12] Many other similar stories could be reproduced here, but I use this extreme example to highlight this strand of *odium sui* in the Christian tradition. For some, self-hatred has meant abolishing any sense of self, any desires of the heart, and make God the only reality, thereby annihilating anything creaturely.[13]

This is not at all Augustine's understanding of self-hatred. While language of self-denial is quite natural in Augustine's writing and preaching, it means something entirely different, referring to our need to ensure we are loving rightly and in a way that unites us with God and neighbor, saving us from collapsing into ourselves and becoming even less than human:

> Where are you now, you that were busy loving yourself? Obviously you're outside. Are you, I'm asking you, are you money? Obviously, after loving yourself by neglecting God, by loving money you have even abandoned yourself. First you have abandoned, and then later on you have destroyed yourself (*Prius deseruisti, postea perdidisti*) ... But you do this because by leaving God out of your life and loving yourself, you have also gone away from yourself; and you now value other things, which are outside you, more than yourself. Come back to yourself; but again, turn upward when you've come back to yourself, don't stay in yourself. First come back to yourself from the things outside you, and then give yourself back to the one who made you, and when you were lost sought you, and as a runaway found you, and when you had turned away turned you back to himself. So then, come back to yourself, and go on to the one who made you ... That is what denying oneself means.[14]

---

[12]Cassian, *Institutes* 4.27, trans., Boniface Ramsey (Mahwah, NJ: Paulist Press, 2000) 92–3.

[13]For more instances of this stern-mindedness, see my "The Dual-Function of the Imago Dei as the Key to Human Flourishing in the Church Fathers," *Ashgate Research Companion to Theological Anthropology*, eds., Joshua Farris and Charles Taliaferro (London: Ashgate, 2015) 191–205.

[14]*s.* 330.3; Hill, *Sermons* (III/9) 186–7.

This is the beginning of atonement, the rejection of all that is not in Christ and letting go of the familiar but fallen sense that in our sins he casts us off. In these places where he contrasts our infidelity and ugliness with God's beautiful faithfulness, Augustine wants us to see that God loves us not despite our sins but precisely because of them. For these wounds he has come to earth.

In his unmatchable way, the great twentieth-century theologian Hans Urs von Balthasar (1905–88) detected this sense of self-loathing as our most prized possession. The acerbic pleasure found in loving oneself wrongly is a sort of security, a stronghold on at least something. Here I need not open up, I need not reveal my despair and dissatisfaction. But it is precisely for this God himself not only takes on a human heart but allows it to be pierced out of love for broken humanity:

> You withdraw into your sorrow: this, at least, is yours. In the experience of your woes you feel yourself alive ... But since you are so wounded, and the open torment of your heart has opened up the abyss of your very self, put out your hand to me and, with it, feel the pulse of another Heart: through this new experience your soul will surrender and heave up the dark gall which it has long collected. I must overpower you. I cannot spare exacting from you your melancholy—your most-loved possession. Give it to me, even if your inner-self thinks it must die. Give me this idol, this cold stony clot in your breast and in its place I will give you a new heart of flesh that will beat to the pulse of my own Heart. Give me this self of yours, which lives on its not being able to live, which is sick because it cannot die. Let it perish, and you will finally begin to live! Dare to leap into the light. Do not take the world to be more profound than God. What could be simpler and sweeter than opening the door of love? What could be easier than falling to one's knees and saying, 'My Lord and my God?'[15]

Is this why Augustine loved his own ruin? It was his own fabricated idol and no one else's, and in this own sovereignty was as close to him as his own stony heart. Are we too embarrassed to admit that we have desecrated God's temple, our own souls, and in that shame do we (like Adam and Eve

---

[15]Hans Urs von Balthasar, *Heart of the World*, trans. Erasmo Leiva (San Francisco: Ignatius Press [1954] 1997) 164–5.

hiding at Gen 3:10) feel a need to distance ourselves from God's piercing gaze? Did Augustine find his own pain more majestic, more immediate, than God's grace? It may not be glorious to behold, but at least it is wholly his. Why risk relationship, why surrender to another, why trust one whom I cannot also control? I may be in ruin, but it is nonetheless wholly my ruin.

In this way we need not fear our ugliness, as that is precisely what God himself took on in the Son's Incarnation. What does this say about God that he decides to woo us into communion through crucifixion? What are we to learn about love standing under the cross, watching the very lifeblood of Love drain away? Augustine's insight into this vulnerability is to see our own woundedness healed and even made beautiful there: "Christ's deformity is what gives form to you. If he had been unwilling to be deformed, you would never have got back the form you lost. So he hung on the cross, deformed; but his deformity was our beauty."[16] This is why our pastor holds up the mortal Christ as a mirror: the lowliness of the perfect God made perfect man is the one who best reflects the human condition. Beholding the blood of our wounds on the blood of the cross, seeing our scars in Christ's own hands and side heals those places where we feel unworthy of love and understanding. By no longer dwelling on our ugliness but offering it to the beautiful Christ, we too become beautiful and glorious to behold. It is typical of Augustine the pastor to look for ways to use the heart's lovesickness and various failures to goad each of us to the loving Christ. Through this process of dual identification, looking at our own wounds we see the lowliness of the Son on the cross. Confession is what unites us, bringing to Christ the ugliness we need him to behold and beautify. Confession to Christ breaks us out of our self-imposed alienation and consequent loathing, for only Christ is able to offer the peace we seek and only his kenosis can empty us of our false selves.

God becomes neighbor, neighbor becomes god

While it is true that Christ's death on the cross paid a debt to Satan incurred by human disobedience, Augustine's atonement theory is much more than simply snatching sinners from the enemy. Rather, Augustinian

---

[16] s. 27.6; Hill, *Sermons* (III/2) 107.

atonement ultimately transforms the unfaithful into the one who alone is just, as Christians become Christ in the latter's merciful descent into sinful humanity. While the passion and cross is of course a central component in this process of identification, the cross is nonetheless one moment among others and cannot really be understood without Bethlehem's manger or Easter Morning's empty tomb.

That does not mean what Augustine has to say about Calvary is irrelevant of course; in fact, his description of the cross as a *muscupula diaboli* in his sermons is wonderful, as the wood is depicted as the devil's "mouse trap" and the body of Christ is the bait that will force the ancient enemy to forego his claim on those close to that cross.

> Along came the redeemer and conquered the deceiver ... To pay our price he set the mousetrap of his cross; as bait he placed there his own blood. While the devil, though, was able to shed that blood, he did not earn the right to drink it. And because he shed the blood of the one who was not his debtor, he was ordered to release those who were his debtors; he shed the blood of the innocent one, he was required to withdraw from those who are by no means innocent.[17]

The enemy forgoes his hold over sinful humanity by unjustly snatching the one truly just man. This blood he did not deserve to drink (*non meruit bibere*). The debt is now paid; sinful humanity's captivity is over. Christ's act of propitiation on the cross is the ultimate sacrifice, freely undertaken for humanity's disobedience.

While these traditional categories of warfare, debt, payment, cross, and eternal claims appear in Augustine's images of atonement, his fuller vision of the cross and its effects on those who draw near to Calvary refuses to be exhausted by one single model. For the question Augustine's theology of atonement ultimately begs is *not to whom does one belong*, but *as who will one eternally be*? Augustine's theology of atonement acts as a bridge connecting two opposite extremes separated by a direly deep chasm. On one side of the chasm stands sinful humanity, self-centered, habitually concupiscent children of Adam, and opposite them stands the crucified and risen Christ whose loving countenance seeks to woo the sinner ever closer. In this way Augustine seeks to make sense of how Christ's sacrificial life and death effect a transformation in sinners. To understand this better, let

---

[17]*s*. 130.2; Hill, *Sermons* (III/4) 311.

us now turn to these three moments of identification, incorporation, and transformation.

Identification

The first step in Augustinian atonement theory is a two fold identification: (1) fallen humans must first identify themselves as sinful (2) and, only then are we able to identify how the crucified Christ has become ugly for the sake of sinners' beauty. "Christ had taken the identity of the first human being to himself ... for it is by longing for him and imitating his passion that we are made new."[18] Since such identity formation for Bishop Augustine is a matter of deep personal introspection fostered best through the silence and ritual of Christian worship, it is not surprising to find most of his theology of atoning identity in his sermons. Liturgy is where and how the truest look at ourselves can be realized.

In *Augustine and the Cure of Souls*, Paul Kolbet examines Augustine's homiletical practices and argues that the Bishop of Hippo "crafted his sermons to involve his hearers in a reflective process whereby the heretofore unperceived blockages that inhibited their self-perception were brought to the surface and articulated."[19] Atonement of sinful humanity to perfect God is achieved by Christ in his passion and resurrection *in toto*, but it is one that demands the graced cooperation of the elect as well. In particular, we see our preacher employ a practice of inviting his flock to return to their experience of brokenness through a use of recapitulative reflection.

We accordingly hear Augustine ask his congregation to allow him to help them see themselves as they truly are: "You blame others, you don't look at yourself; you accuse others, you don't think about yourself; you place others before your eyes, you place yourself behind your back. When I accuse, I do the opposite. I take you from behind your back, and put you down in front of your eyes."[20] Why do people not want to face their truest selves? Because it would mean seeing our own pride and infidelities; but in denying a true examination of our souls, we inevitably eclipse God from acting in our lives as well: "So, those who won't acknowledge the Creator are proudly denying their maker, while those who deny their

---

[18]*en. Ps.* 37.27; Boulding, *Expositions* (III/16) 166.
[19]Paul R. Kolbet, *Augustine and the Cure of Souls* (Notre Dame, IN: Notre Dame University Press, 2010) 182.
[20]*s.*17.5; Hill, *Sermons* (III/1) 369.

sickness don't acknowledge the necessity of a savior. So let us both praise the Creator for our nature, and for the flaw in it which we have inflicted on ourselves."[21]

Through this art of returning to—and being thankful for—our self-inflicted wounds, Augustine employs a style of homiletic recapitulation which tends to follow a four fold rhetorical pattern as such:

(1) The initial prompt for the congregation to examine some experience in their lives. Through certain exhortatory prompts like *redeamus* ("let us now return") or *exspectemus* ("what it is we await"), Augustine invites his people to reflect on what it is they lack, hope for, or desire;

(2) Next comes the clear and unabashed introduction of Jesus Christ as the sole solution or antidote to the restlessness just visited;

(3) Augustine next illustrates how the Son descends into each sinner's deficiency by means of his own divine humanity, utilizing various metaphors to illustrate how the Lord will make himself real in the lives of those present;

(4) This results in the fourth stage and the subsequent atoning and final transformation of that former condition, that initial prompt of introspection.

Augustine often begins these recapitulative tropes by employing key phrases obviously dear to him, hortatory subjunctives prompting parishioners to look more deeply into their own hearts to see there what it is they have experienced or for what it is they hope. Such "polite commands" aim to capitalize on the congregation's innate desire for a life other than what they find themselves living for on any given Sunday morning.

For example, we are able to trace these four recapitulative elements in most sermons where Bishop Augustine invite his congregants to examine their souls: (1) "So let's go back (*redeamus*) and listen ... and take a look at ourselves (*inspiciamus nos*) and anything we find defective in ourselves, let us work at putting right with all diligence ... (2) May the one who formed us reform us, (3) the one who created us recreate us, the one who installed us (4) restore us to perfection."[22] Returning to their true selves, Augustine's congregation is asked to look honestly at whatever brokenness (*quidquid*

---

[21] *s.* 156.2; Hill, *Sermons* (III/5) 97.
[22] *s.* 301A.2; Hill, *Sermons* (III/8) 291.

deesse inuenerimus) they may find within themselves so as to let God know and heal them there. Here we catch a glimpse of the love of a pastor refusing to shy away from a bit of discomfort in exposing defects, so as to let the Lord work more promptly and effectively. This is a manner of prompting Augustine utilizes often: "Take a look at yourselves, go back (*redite*) to your consciences, interrogate your faith, interrogate your love."[23] By inviting his flock to go back and search their previous experiences, Augustine the preacher is employing a form of psychagogy, trusting that the Gospel becomes more alive when its interlocutors first sense their own desperation alongside their absolute need for a savior to come to them.

At one point he has his congregation meditate on the power of God: "Be still (*uacate*). To what purpose? And see that I am God. See that you are not God, but I am. I created you, and I recreate you; I formed you, and I form you anew; I made you, and I remake you. If you had no power to make yourself, how do you propose to remake yourself?"[24] At other times, such a couplet becomes a prayer: "May the one who formed us, reform us, the one who created us recreate us, the one who installed us restore us to perfection."[25] The same God who creates humanity is the same God who redeems humanity: unlike the Manichean separation between maker and redeemer, creator and savior, the Christian God enters his own creation to reverse the narrative of disobedience.

Given the dualism Augustine found so attractive as a Manichean, it should not surprise us to see how he very early in his preaching stresses the unity of God not only immanently but even more pastorally significant economically. This is the first effect using the movement of recapitulation has in one of Augustine's sermons and reveals a consistent Augustinian principle, namely that God longs to amend rather than end that which is imperfect. "He didn't, after all, make us and now desert us. He didn't go to the trouble of making us, and then not bother to look after us."[26] God did not create an individual with all of his or her individual histories and heart's desires, personalities, and character traits, simply to dismiss and deny such unique individuality. God created each of us in the way he did in order to save each in his or her own particular manner as well. This is far from any Manichean dualism: there is not one God who fashioned a fallen self and

---

[23]*s.* 73A; Hill, *Sermons* (III/3) 296; cf. *Jo. eu. tr.* 18.5.
[24]*en. Ps.* 45.14; Boulding, *Expositions* (III/16) 322.
[25]*s.* 301A; Hill, *Sermons* (III/8) 291.
[26]*s.* 26.1; Hill, *Sermons* (III/2) 93.

another God who aims to liberate that historical being, but one God who like a loving Father raised us slowly, beginning with creation and then the law and then the fullness of love in the sending of his Son.

In fact, this is how the Father persuades us (*persuadendum*) of his love, thereby assuring us that his love is greater than our sins. Through the Son's humility on the cross, God shows us simultaneously both his care as well as our own wretchedness: the cross displays his love so we know our worth; it reveals our sins so we desist in our pride.

> First we had to be persuaded how much God loved us, in case out of sheer despair we lacked the courage to reach up to him. Also we had to be shown what sort of people we are that he loves, in case we should take pride in our own worth, and so bounce even further away from him and sink even more under our own strength. So he dealt with us in such a way that we could progress rather in his strength; he arranged it so that the power of charity would be brought to perfection in the weakness of humility.[27]

In holding up the bloody and mortal Christ as a mirror of our human condition, Augustine wants to show us how our own wounds are healed. In this identification he invites sinful humanity to see its own ugliness now made beautiful in Christ. Beholding Calvary's bloodied corpse enables us to see the toxicity of our own concupiscence which placed Christ there. If we remain stuck in our pride, we will never be able to see the glory and beauty of the cross; but if we allow grace to find our own deformities displeasing, we will receive Christ's own beauty precisely there. This sort of identifying our haughtiness with Christ's lowliness leads to our incorporation into Christ. Through operative grace, the sinner stops seeking to flee and finally offers him or herself to God. Here one receives God's own self, as Christ extends his very life to make the faithful into other sons and daughters.[28]

Incorporation

To show how God uses the experiences of our lives to draw us to himself, Augustine most often relies on a rich image of the "whole Christ"

---

[27] *Trin.* 4.2; Hill, *The Trinity* (I/5) 153.
[28] For further study into identity: *s.* 73A; *Trin.* 4 and 13; *f. et symb.* 4.6; *uera rel.* §16.32; *cat. rud.* §48.

(*Christus totus*), his method of showing how Jesus the Head chooses to identify himself with his Body the Church. This is an essential move in understanding Augustinian atonement because love always identifies with the beloved. That is, in his love for sinners, Christ neither glosses over the grave condition of sinners, nor does he simply forgive from afar. In his self-emptying, the incarnate Son becomes one with all of humanity and in this assumption of the human condition, all can see in Christ his or her own humanity. Most often this type of identification appears whenever Augustine uses various lines from Matthew 25 ("Whatever you do to the least of these, you do to me ...") or Acts 9:4 ("Saul, Saul, why do you persecute me?"). Inevitably, Augustine will use these two loci to depict the extension of Christ's own heavenly body into his mystical body on earth. For example, notice the casual movement from identification ("look at ourselves") to incorporation where our truest identity is the "whole Christ," head and body:

> Now, however, I wonder if we shouldn't have a look at ourselves, if we shouldn't think about his body, because he is also us (*quia et nos ipse est*). After all, if we weren't him, this wouldn't be true: *When you did it for one of the least of mine, you did it for me* (Mt 25:40). If we weren't him, this wouldn't be true: *Saul, Saul, why are you persecuting me?* (Acts 9:4). So we too are him, because we are his organs, because we are his body, because he is our head, because the whole Christ is both head and body.[29]

This incorporation of Christians into Christ is effected in the sacrifice of the Eucharist, where Augustine tells his faithful, the Body of Christ, to see their own lives on the altar: "it's the mystery meaning you that has been placed on the Lord's table; what you receive is the mystery that means you."[30]

Most of Augustine's reflections on the atoning power of charity are found in his homilies on St. John's Gospel and Epistles, the canonical texts to which he turned in order to combat the ever-divisive Donatists. The unity which grace effects not only atones for the most dastardly of repentant sinners (something the Donatist could not allow), thereby bringing him or her back into ecclesial communion, it makes one into another Christ:

---

[29] *s.* 133.8; Hill, *Sermons* (III/4) 338; *s.* 263A.2; *en. Ps.* 21.3, 40.6.
[30] *s.* 272; Hill, *Sermons* (III/7) 300; *Jo. eu. tr.* 26.13–18.

Let us congratulate ourselves then and give thanks for having been made not only Christians but Christ. Do you understand, brothers and sisters, the grace of God upon us; do you grasp that? Be filled with wonder, rejoice and be glad; we have been made Christ. For if he is the head, and we the members, then he and we are the whole man ... The fullness of Christ, then, is the head and the members. What is that, head and members? Christ and the Church.[31]

Atonement is an ecclesial reality for Augustine: the stress he gives is on how Christ saves his people, his body, and not just disparate individuals. The Church is where and how God's people are brought out of their sinful self-centeredness and adopted into his own life. To be an atoned sinner is simply not to become a Christian, it is to become Christ, as his sacred humanity not only affects ours but becomes ours.[32]

Transformation

Incorporation is inevitably transformative and that is why atonement for Augustine ultimately means deification. The oneness achieved through the incarnate Son's physical death for our spiritual death not only awakens our soul but divinizes us into new creatures—adopted children of the Father, coheirs with Christ, temples of the Holy Spirit. This is why Augustinian atonement is much richer than standard accounts appreciate: it bridges the heart's ultimate desire with the greatest promise God could possibly make a creature:

We carry mortality about with us, we endure infirmity, we look forward to divinity. For God wishes not only to vivify, but also to deify us. When would human infirmity ever have dared to hope for this, unless divine truth had promised it? ... Still, it was not enough for our God to promise us divinity in himself, unless he also took on our infirmity, as though to say, "Do you want to know how much I love you, how certain you ought to be that I am going to give you my divine reality? I took to myself your mortal reality." We mustn't find it incredible, brothers and sisters, that human beings become gods, that is, that those who were human beings become gods.[33]

---

[31]*Jo. eu. tr.* 21.8; Hill, *Homilies on the Gospel of John* (I/12) 379.
[32]For further study into incorporation: *s.* 15, 115, 166, 337, 341; *ciu. Dei*, 10.6, 19.23; *en. Ps.* 26, *exp.* 2.2, 40.6; *Jo. eu. tr.* 108.5.
[33]*s.* 23B.1, Hill, *Sermons* (III/11) 37.

Since justification leads to divinization (synonymous realities in Augustine's mind),[34] he always sets Christ's atoning work in a larger picture of our deifying transformation: God becomes human and undergoes the toxic effects of our disobedience on the cross in order to turn us into his own brothers and sisters.

While Augustine has no problem calling the elect "gods" or "other Christs," he most often draws from originally Pauline "great exchange" imagery (e.g., 2 Cor 8:9) to describe how atonement occurs. On the cross God exchanges his weakness for our power. That is why the bishop exhorts his flock to appreciate the vulnerability which first unites God to sinners, thus pointing to the weakness of the crucified one: "There you have something for your infirmity, something for your becoming perfect. Let Christ set you on your feet by that in him which is man, let him lead you forward by that in him which is Godman, let him lead you right through to that which is God."[35] This is the purpose of the Incarnation as a whole and the cross in particular, to transform the sinner into a saint.

That is why the great convert never shies away from reflecting on human weakness, because the incarnate Lord himself never shies away from it: "we should not find it surprising that to meet our weakness he descended to the discrete sounds we use, for he also descended to take to himself the weakness of our human body."[36] Or we hear later:

> We could not grasp his divinity, if he had not put on our mortality and come down to us to announce the gospel to us, if he had been unwilling to share with us what in us is base and of no importance, we would have thought that the one who took our smallness upon himself was unwilling to give us his greatness.[37]

We thus see how fallen human qualities, such as bodily frailty (*infirmitas corporis*) or human mortality, are taken up (*ad suscipiendam*) by the Son's Incarnation and, in return, are replaced with Christ's own integrity and immortality.

The cross of Christ establishes a unity between the immortal and the mortal in his very self, "aiming later on to give us shares in himself, having

---

[34]This is the argument I make in my *The One Christ: St. Augustine's Theology of Deification* (Washington, DC: Catholic University of America Press, 2013).

[35]*Jo. eu. tr.* 23.6; Hill, *Homilies on the Gospel of John* (I/12) 410.

[36]*en. Ps.* 103, *exp.* 4.1; Boulding, *Expositions* (III/19) 167; cf. *en. Ps.* 102.22; *en. Ps.* 33, *exp.* 1.6.

[37]*Jo. eu. tr.* 22.1; Hill, *Homilies on the Gospel of John* (I/12) 389.

first of all himself taken shares in us. I mean, we had nothing of our very own by which we could really live, and he had nothing of his very own by which he could really die. Accordingly, he struck a wonderful bargain with us, a mutual give and take; ours was what he died by; his is what we might live by."[38]

Augustine is careful not to verge on pantheism or to violate the divine nature in any way, as one of his most consistent pleas is to insist how divine interaction with creation changes only the created while divinity goes unaltered: "Because the Word was made flesh it was the very Word himself who was crucified, but the Word was not changed into humanity; rather, humanity was changed by its union with him. Human nature was changed in him to become nobler (*melior*) than it had been before, but it was not changed into the substance of the Word."[39] So, when Mary said "yes" at the Annunciation, it was humanity assumed and joined to God. It was not the divine that changed, but the human.

Augustine's rhetorical training provided him with a most apt image for this moment of unique transformation when Mary spoke her *fiat*. When one speaks a word, it is not the invisible and immaterial word in the mind that changes. Rather, it is the materiality assumed to that mental word—the air of one's lungs, the lips, tongue and other necessary oral tissue, etc. … — which changes. In such an act of speech, the word in the mind remains transcendent and unchanged; it is the material components needed for speaking that are properly adjusted and adapted in order to make that otherwise inaudible, insensible word known in the world of time and space. At Mary's "yes," therefore, it was not the Word who changed, but it was the humanity of the New Eve and, by extension, the humanity of all her children. As Augustine would envision it, at that moment of the Annunciation, it was not the divinity of God which changed, but the humanity of creatures that is eternally perfected.[40] This is the moment when earth and heaven, God and humanity, become one. Accordingly, Augustine is now able to stress how the lowliness of the earthly Christ renders us into godly creatures: "You were [children] of men and you have become (*estis facti*) [children] of God. He has shared with us our ills, and he is going to give us his goods."[41] This deifying sort of imagery reveals how Jesus Christ's death offers much more

---

[38]*s.* 218C.1; Hill, *Sermons* (III/6) 194.

[39]*en. Ps.* 130.10; Boulding, *Expositions* (III/20) 148.

[40]This is most clearly worked out in *Trin.* 15.19.20; Hill, *The Trinity*, 409–10, but can also be seen whenever Augustine contrasts the immaterial, eternal Logos with the words spoken in time.

[41]*s.* 121.5; Hill, *Sermons* (III/4) 236, slightly adjusted.

than instruction or moral improvement. The atoning work of Christ may begin by justifying the sinner and removing the concupiscence he or she once so freely embraced, but it ends in the divinizing elevation of mortals into immorality, of humans into divinity, of sinners into saints.

Unification of loves

The third and final effect of Christ's atoning work is the identification of love of God and love of neighbor. If God in fact has become our neighbor, Augustine will comfort his people by assuring them that if they love their spouses, children and grandchildren, and their friends rightly in Christ, they are loving them with God's very self, and as a result, *love cannot be separated.* What assurance it must have been to hear the great orator Augustine assure his people that they were not to divide their loves into sacred and secular, into a pious love of God when attending church, and another love throughout the week for the more mundane. He accordingly asks:

> How can that be when you love Christ's members? When you love Christ's members, then, you love Christ; when you love Christ, you love the Son of God; when you love the Son of God, you also love his Father. Love, then, cannot be separated. Choose for yourself what to love; others come to you as a result. Should you say, "I love God alone, God the Father," you are lying. If you love, you don't love one thing alone, but, if you love the Father, you also love the Son … and if you love the head, you also love the members … the Church itself.[42]

Love cannot be separated because charity and Christ are one. But Augustine was not always so reassuring. He matured into this position, having lived out many years of his vocation as pastor and curator of souls appreciating firsthand the indivisibility of charity.

In 393 Augustine—a young and promising priest, ordained not even two years prior—is invited to preach to the bishops of North Africa gathered at the general Synod of Hippo. In his discourse Augustine naturally and easily turns to the topic of God as love, and for the first time in his public career looks at 1 Jn 4:8, that *God is love.* Before these attending bishops Augustine was adamant that the Apostle John wrote that God is love

---

[42]*ep. Jo.* 10.3; Ramsey, *Homilies on the First Epistle of John* (I/14) 148.

because he also wanted simultaneously to teach that clearly love is not God: "The scriptures do not say, *Love is God*, but that *God is love*, which," Augustine insists, "means that divinity alone is to be loved" (*etiam hic enim non ait: Dilectio Deus est; sed Deus dilectio est; ut ipsa deitas dilectio intellegatur*).[43]

Imagine the scene: the brightest as well as the most mischievous kid in his class returns to his homeland, now ordained as one of Christ's priests, is asked to address the leading bishops in his recently embraced Church. For the first time Augustine of Hippo, a man who left these shores with a concubine and small child—now both gone—went to work for the emperor at the recommendation of Quintus Aurelius Symmachus, archenemy of the great Ambrose and the Roman Church. This young cleric realizes he is known to this collection of ecclesial dignitaries as someone who spent almost a decade as a professed enemy of Christianity, but who is now able publicly to defend the sincerity of his love for Christ and his ecclesia. Perhaps desirous of showing how all earthly eros and worldly desire have been eradicated in him, the relatively new convert zealously pronounces that scripture quite clearly holds how God alone is love, so God alone can be loved.

Yet almost fifteen years later, both Augustine's interior life as well as the demands of his public office had changed considerably. By the year 407 he has proven himself a successful and faithful bishop, he has spent countless hours listening to the pains and the promises of thousands of simple believers, he has preached, heard confessions, and spent long days adjudicating civil court cases. So the next time he turns back to comment on this same passage of the First Epistle of John, he not only inverts the taxonomy here but even attributes this reversal to the Evangelist himself.

In his *Homilies on the First Epistle of John*, delivered in the Easter season of 407, we accordingly hear:

> How, then, could it be a short while ago, Love is from God, and now Love is God? For God is the Father and Son and Holy Spirit. The Son is God from God, the Holy Spirit is God from God, and these three are one God, not three gods. If the Son is God and the Holy Spirit is God, and he loves him in whom the Holy Spirit dwells, then *love is God*, but it is God because it is from God.[44]

---

[43] *f. et sym.* 9.19; Campbell, *On Christian Belief* (I/8) 170.
[44] *ep. Jo.* 7.6; Ramsey, *Homilies on the First Epistle of John* (I/14) 108.

In this fifteen-year gap between Augustine's exegesis of First John, he has now come to a place where he can state that if God is love, love is God. We again see how the mutual indwelling of the Holy Spirit assures us that what we wish to call love will be God's essence (*est Deus*; 1 Jn 4:8) as well as that movement from and back to God (*ex Deo*; 1 Jn 4:7). This is a position which only grows in the following decades. In a homily dated 419, from which we cited an earlier section above, we again hear how to love and to be loved is a gift of the Holy Spirit and "So, charity being entirely the gift of God to such an extent that it is even called God, as the apostle John says: Charity is God, and whoever remains in charity remains in God and God in him."[45] Notice how Augustine now actually attributes this inversion to the Apostle himself, a convenient slip when he is advancing a rather intriguing innovation.[46]

This authorial inversion was made possibly only because Augustine has matured as a pastor and curator of the human condition. He passes his days counseling and listening, seeing how his congregants love their children and boast about their grandchildren. The residual guilt of misusing his heart and his intellect has subsided; his interaction with the Christian families and farmers of the Mauritanian plains has opened his eyes to the holiness of all loves. The mature Augustine is no longer afraid of two competing kinds of loves, one Christian and one carnal. By now he sees that there is only one love, God, and so, the question of whether one starts with the divine or with the human has been answered. This one love progresses from God to God's people with such clarity and circularity, Augustine can unabashedly encourage his flock with the gentle encouragement that in loving one another truly, they are inevitably loving the Christ. Augustine clearly no longer fears that what is to be properly considered charity can replace God, for it is God. In fact, he tells his congregation, "Love him; whatever you love, it comes from him" (*Ama illum: quidquid amas, ab illo est*).[47]

Not one to shy away from dramatics in the pulpit, oftentimes rehearsing imaginary conversations between believers as we have seen, Augustine draws from a rather common experience from the dusty streets of Hippo

---

[45]*s.* 156.5; Hill, *Sermons* (III/5) 99–100.

[46]For more on this reversal, see T.J. van Bavel, "The Double Face of Love in St. Augustine— The Daring Inversion: Love is God," *Studia Ephemeridis «Augustinianum»* 26:3 (1986) 69–80; Roland Teske, S.J., "Augustine's Inversion of 1 John 4:8," *Augustinian Studies* 39:1 (2008) 49–60; and Raymond Canning, *The Unity of Love for God and Neighbor in St. Augustine* (Heverlee-Leuven: Augustinian Historical Institute, 1993).

[47]*s.* 261.4; Hill, *Sermons* (III/7) 210; *ep. Jo.* 5.7, 9.10; *Trin.* 8.12.

to make a theological point: the exchange between a learned pagan and a new Christian. In a sermon on the Feast of the Lord's Ascension, he has to come to terms with the fact that the incarnate and visible Son of God is now seated at the Father's right hand. He cleverly depicts a non-Christian interlocutor who challenges the neophyte's recently received Creed who in turn responds, "You're saying to me, 'Show me your God,' but I'm saying to you, 'Pay a little attention to your heart.' 'Show me your God,' you say. But I say: 'Attend a little to your heart.'"[48] But in his heart the pagan finds all sorts of sin and filth and thus shies away from the God of the Christian before whom he feels judged and unworthy. Yet this same God bends low to use this moment of true fear to teach that,

> God is too much for you; but God became man. What was a long way away from you has come down right next to you through a man. The place for you to stay in, that's God; the way for you to get there, that's man. It's one and the same Christ, both the way to go by and the place to go to.[49]

In this exchange, we can appreciate a bigger piece of theology than just a missiological method in how to witness to nonbelievers. We see how Augustine understands how most of us have come to love God by first loving humanity.

In other words, he has come to appreciate how the human heart, regardless of geographical nationality or the diversity of personal experience, desires the same end—immortality and joy. That is why his famous line at the opening of his *Confessions* is in the singular: our heart is unsettled, unquiet, *cor nostrum inquietum*—our heart is restless until it rests in Thee, O God. The Christian and the non-Christian have the same heart. This proves to be the locus of evangelization or, as he will preach on another occasion, when you want to teach others of Christ, point them to what gives their hearts pleasure, and in whom they find delight.

Quoting his first intellectual mentor, the Latin poet Virgil, Augustine uses what would be a familiar line to his Latin congregation, "Each one is by his pleasure drawn," from Virgil's *Second Eclogue* (§65). Again leading this flock into deeper reflection on their commitments, obligations, and daily joys, the Bishop of Hippo continues that:

---

[48]*s*. 261.5; Hill, *Sermons* (III/7) 211.
[49]*s*. 261.7; Hill, *Sermons* (III/7) 212.

> Those whose delight is in the truth, whose delight is in happiness, whose delight is in justice, whose delight is in eternal life, are drawn to Christ, because each of those is Christ … Give me a lover, and he will know by experience what I am saying here. Give me a man of desires, give me someone who is hungry, give me someone traveling thirsty through this wilderness and panting for the fountain of eternal life, and he will know what I am saying.[50]

In this way Augustine would have moments of evangelization begin not in lofty dogma but in the desires of the heart, insisting that the Roman and the Christian seeks the same goal of joy, of knowing and being known, loving and being loved. "Give me a lover," someone of deep desires, Augustine cries, assured that true charity cannot help but elevate the lover into Love himself.

For that reason, the formerly suspicious Augustine has come to understand how most of us have come to love. Was it not by gazing upon a smiling face appearing over our cribs? Was it not the love of a mother which incorporated us into the mysteries and levels of charity and care, the love of friends as we grew, the love of a spouse and our own children in whom we found our own hearts expanding? So while the love of a creature may be chronologically and often even emotionally prior, the love of God must be ontologically and formatively first. It is one and the same love but experienced by creatures appropriate to our maturation and life's unfolding.

But there is a caveat and a caution along the way. We hear often from the Bishop's pulpit, that we must love *bene*—love well or correctly—if what we consider to be love will, in the end, be worthy of the name:

> If you recognize it, God is love (1 Jn 4:8.16). So if you have been drinking love, tell me what place you have drunk it in. If you recognize it, if you have seen it, if you love it, what do you love it with? After all, whatever you love rightly (*Quidquid enim bene amas, caritate amas*), you love with love. And how can you love anything with love if you don't love? So if you love it, what do you love it with … That's how you must learn to love God.[51]

Identifying love with God's essence carries obvious expectations. We must love well (*bene*), which is nothing other than loving virtuously. In fact, one

---

[50] *Jo. eu. tr.* 26.4; Hill, *Homilies on the Gospel of John* (I/12) 452–3.
[51] *s.* 23.13; Hill, *Sermons* (II/2) 62.

could easily check such movements with, say, St. Paul's characteristics of charity in 1 Corinthians 13: Love is patient; love is kind; love is never self-seeking; and so on. The truth of the matter for Augustine is that love is an all or nothing event: we either love one another with God's very self which therefore necessitates such love will be unwaveringly virtuous, chaste, and fruitful, or we are bound to one another out of our own fallen fabrications. That is, the glue between each is either the Holy Spirit or it is our own interior poverties—fear, control, lust, or manipulation. Either we have only a tenuous and fleeting connection that death will surely destroy, or we are together as one forever.

Conclusion

Augustine's Christology is all-encompassing. The Son of God becomes human in the womb of the Virgin Mary, but becomes more and more himself in his Church, the "whole Christ" (*Christus totus*), as Christ's members become more and more themselves in him. The imagery Augustine uses to describe this identification is powerful and goes far beyond the justification of sinners achieved at Calvary. Christians are to become Christ; they are to assent to themselves being the Body of Christ every time they receive Holy Communion, and so on. In his vulnerability, Christ assumes to himself what he needs to die in order to give to us a share in what we need to live. The Son's kenosis becomes the theosis of innumerable sons and daughters.

In this at-one-ment, the world is therefore no longer hostilely divided between God and humanity, between spirit and matter, light and dark. The pernicious dualism of the Manicheans has been unified in the power of the Trinity who pursues even the most faithless. In the Son's Incarnation, contraries have become Christified. Hereafter, to be first is to be last, to live is to die, and to love God is to love your neighbor as yourself. Surrendering to this mortally enfleshed God is now the sole way out of our various forms of self-destruction. Only in him do we need not fear our brokenness or punish ourselves for our unfaithfulness. Here is a God who longs to console his people from the cross, to win them over not through strength and perfection which they could never achieve, but through a vulnerability and weakness they know all too well.

CONCLUSION

Soul, self; come, poor Jackself, I do advise
You, jaded, let be; call off thoughts awhile
Elsewhere; leave comfort root-room; let joy size
At God knows when to God knows what; whose smile
's not wrung, see you; unforeseen times rather—as skies
Between pie mountains—lights a lovely mile.[1]

The overall thesis of these chapters has been to argue that underneath the warped actions of the fallen soul, that before any visible maliciousness lies a chronic pull to our own self-harm. These pages have sought to understand why Augustine's pilfering of pears tugged at him so intensely so many years later. The answer I propose is that before any actual sin is made manifest, there is a nagging yet persistent voice within every fallen soul that one is not worthy of wholeness. There thus arises an acid pleasure of engaging the forbidden. We shut out everyone else so we can become God, perversely imitating the omnipotence under which we know we must live. This is the first fruit of Adam's sin: in our concupiscence, our God-given desire for otherness becomes rotten. Our need to be loved is perceived as a dangerous threat. This is why Augustine was at first simply in love with love—some abstract thrill, pursuit, and desire for attaining at least a semblance for what he has been created. "What was it that delighted me? Only loving and being loved ..."[2] Augustine knows that he cannot not desire to love, but instead of risking a relationship which exposes and eternalizes, this young lover chooses a fictive love projected from his own inescapable need for communion, a fabrication of intimacy that will result only in dissolution and destruction.

---

[1]Gerard Manley Hopkins, S.J., second stanza of "My own heart let me more have pity on," *The Poems of Gerard Manley Hopkins*, ed., W.H. Gardner and N.H. MacKenzie (Oxford: Oxford University Press, 1967) 102.
[2]*conf.* 2.1.1; Boulding, *Confessions* (I/1) 62.

This is how sin has been presented in these pages: a freely chosen autonomy and alienation, resulting in the loathing and ruin of self. In other words, we sin when we remove ourselves from interpersonal communion and inevitably establish ourselves as our own sovereigns, thereby producing the sort of self that needs to be destroyed. For Augustine, sin produces internal fragmentation and the divided will rebels against itself, intent not only on distance from the Good but destruction of any Good that demands the soul's allegiance. Such sin for Augustine is a way of keeping others—the only source of our healing—at a safe distance. Unwilling to entrust himself to another, Augustine learned early on that senseless acts of violence, perverted sexuality, a condescending demeanor, and even cruel words were ways he could never be asked to submit truly to another. Sabotaging himself through his own sins allowed him to stay at the center of his world, never having to be jeopardized by allowing another to become important to him. The recklessness of sin extinguishes the demands of closeness. Yet in such extinguishing, a level of self-hatred arises that even Augustine found difficult to articulate. The shame of sin initiates a vicious circle, beginning with the fall of Satan, the enticement of Adam and Eve, and the original sinfulness that every human thereafter effects in his or her own concupiscence.

When examining a relatively harmless offense of his teenage years, Augustine admits that this deed remained worthy of confession because it was as close to the abyss of nothingness as a soul could wander. His intention in stealing those pears was never to satisfy his physical hunger, but to deepen the crevice of self-loathing that had already fractured his heart. In love with his own ruin, he was still unwilling to confess that God's love was greater than human misery. As a result, our searcher refused to place himself in the Son's pierced hands, and instead attempted to love himself by himself. Selfishly turned in on himself, then, he relished his own decay, and sweetened it all the more through senseless acts of ruin. Augustine sought to destroy himself because at least it was *he* who was doing it. Such ruin attracts our divided selves because now the demands of goodness are dismissed, and the riskiness of relationship is relinquished. We seek to become godly without God.

After the thrill of this senseless act, Augustine came to see that what he had been choosing was not the specious beauty of the pears themselves but was instead choosing his own self as the source of his security. Augustine, not the pears, had become the idol which had to be shattered. This is the double-mindedness Augustine's psychology of sin reveals: in sin we are alienated against our own selves because we are both drawn to and repulsed by goodness. We long for love but we want love on our own terms. The primordial battle continues in every soul, this war between solipsism and surrender. The Christian scriptures therefore advise us to hate ourselves, to deny ourselves. But this is to be done in Christ, not out of a self-loathing that is in love with its own ruin, but out of the graced awareness that we are to hate the foolishness (*stultum*) that we are incapable of perfection:

> Let them love wise and perfect souls for being such as they see them to be, foolish ones not for being such but because they are capable of being perfect and wise, since they should not even love themselves as being foolish. I mean, those who love themselves as being foolish will make no progress towards wisdom, nor will any become what they long to be unless they hate what they are.[3]

In Christ we are capable of perfection, a renewed wholeness achieved only through the mutual indwelling achieved by divine union.

Augustine assumes that any human can detect a scintilla of love for another in his or her life, and this is where the healing begins. Love is not simply instinct or nostalgia. Let it be discerned as divine charity, as the place where God is allowed to begin to act. In fact, when this happens one begins to understand that all love is divine; there is no such thing as human charity for Augustine. There is no longer a false distinction between a secular love and a sanctifying love. This is what our author realized when he fell on Christ in another garden years later. Here he came to realize how powerfully and tenderly he was sought, how he was divinely desired. In such assurance of love does the risk of relationship subside. Here we can allow ourselves to be known, healed, and loved. In becoming our poor and persecuted brother and sister, God becomes the love we know we have for our friends and spouses, our children, grandchildren, and ourselves: "Amen, I say to you, whatever you did for one of these least brothers or sisters of mine, you did for me" (Mt 25:40).

This is the beginning of all Christian kerygma, that the sinner—as prodigal as he or she proves to be—is in fact eternally and perfectly loved: "there is quite obviously no stronger motive for love, either in its initial stages or in its growth, that for the person who does not yet love to discover that he is loved, and for the person who is first to love to hope that his love can be reciprocated or to have clear signs that it already is so."[4] Why surrender to one

---

[3] *uera rel.* 48.93; Hill, *On True Religion*, as in *On Christian Belief* (I/8) 92.
[4] *cat. rud.* 1.4.7; Canning, *Instructing Beginners in the Faith* (I/10) 68.

who does not love perfectly? Why love another who refuses to reciprocate my entrustment of self? On the cross these questions are answered:

> Christ the way is the humble Christ; Christ the truth and the life is Christ exalted and God. If you walk along the humble Christ, you will arrive at the exalted Christ; if in your sickly health and debility you do not spurn the humble one, you will abide in the perfect health and strength with the exalted one. What else, after all, was the reason for Christ's humility, but your debility?[5]

The greatness of God is calibrated to mortal sinners through the abasement of the Christ. On the cross we see the life-giving power of vulnerability and the lesson for the whole human race to entrust ourselves into the hands of another, regardless of the dangers of love.

Augustine of Hippo spent his entire priestly life trying to bring this awareness to others. Despite the allures of this good creation, he knew the loneliness of a life spent only for oneself. In Christ's Church he found the community and the eternity which he sought. It was here in the crucified but hopeful Body of Christ on earth that he found his own worth and was given the grace to overcome the hatred he festered for his sinful self. This was his true self, freed from having to act furtively and manipulatively under the cover of darkness, and now united to the perfect man, Jesus Christ. Phrases running throughout Augustine's Christology like "we are he" (*nos ipse*) or "we are in him" (*sumus in illo*), signal this wholeness, "because in me they are also I" (*quoniam in me etiam ipsi sunt ego*). This is charity incarnate, where the Lover assumes his beloved to himself, thereby making the end of self-harm finally possible. Stopping all hatred and mending all destruction, the Whole Christ becomes the place of true healing, where the community of the sanctified can not only be forgiven but begin to forgive themselves and one another as well.

Once he was living in Christ, Augustine came to realize that his unquiet heart was not made to live on self-harm and disappointment, but on a God made weak whose own pierced heart was the only way to wholeness. No one ever starts out intending his or her own destruction. Yet through repeated disappointments, sustained neglect, and the denigration our own sins inevitably bring, any one of us can come to treat ourselves maliciously. We can fall in love with our own ruin. Yet the mystery of sin is that we

---

[5] *s.* 142.2; Hill, *Sermons* (III/4) 413–14.

never choose evil only because it is evil.[6] But as creatures with the majestic gift of free will, we can choose the slightest scintilla of being, any tenebrous shade promising some level of light, however faint. For those who have known only abuse and disappointment, the mere exertion of their wills—for whatever reason, toward whatever object (even lackluster fruit!)—and their mere "choosing" can quickly become their god. This idol may take the form of a pear, of another human body, of intellectual superiority, and Augustine had worshipped them all. But God descends as one of us to show us our eternal worth, his own infinite love shining in and through us, having used his own body and blood to convince each of us how much we are loved.

---

[6]This is clearly the Thomistic position as well, see *Summa Theologiae* I–II 72.1.

FURTHER READING

Auerbach, Eric ([1953] 1991), *Mimesis: The Representation of Reality in Western Literature*, Princeton: Princeton University Press.

von Balthasar, Hans Urs ([1954] 1997), *Heart of the World*, trans. Erasmo Leiva, San Francisco: Ignatius Press.

van Bavel, Tarcisius (1986), "The Double Face of Love in St. Augustine—The Daring Inversion: Love Is God," *Studia Ephemeridis "Augustinianum"* 26:3, 69–80.

Bergoglio, Jorge Mario ([2005] 2013), *The Way of Humility: Corruption and Sin, On Self-Accusation*, San Francisco: Ignatius Press.

Cacioppo, John T. and William Patrick (2008), *Loneliness: Human Nature and the Need for Social Connection*, New York: W. W. Norton & Co.

Canning, Raymond (1993), *The Unity of Love for God and Neighbor in St. Augustine*, Heverlee-Leuven: Augustinian Historical Institute.

Capps, Donald (2007), "Augustine's Confessions: Self-Reproach and the Melancholy Self," *Pastoral Psychology* 55, 571–91.

Cavadini, John (2007), "The Darkest Enigma: Reconsidering the Self in Augustine's Thought," *Augustinian Studies* 38, 119–32.

Clark, Mary (1994), *Augustine*, London: Geoffrey Chapman.

Congar, O.P., Yves ([1979–80] 1997), *I Believe in the Holy Spirit*, trans. David Smith, New York: Crossroad Publishing.

Groeschel, Benedict, C.F.R. (1983), *Spiritual Passages: The Psychology of Spiritual Development*, New York: Crossroad Publishing.

Kohut, Heinz (1971), *The Analysis of the Self: A Systematic Approach to the Psychoanalytic Treatment of Narcissistic Personality Disorders*, New York: International Universities Press.

Kolbet, Paul R. (2010), *Augustine and the Cure of Souls*, Notre Dame, IN: Notre Dame University Press.

Ladaria, Louis F. (2010), *The Living and True God: The Mystery of the Trinity*, New York: Convivium Press.

Lasch, Christopher (1979), *The Culture of Narcissism: American Life in an Age of Diminishing Expectations*, New York: Warner Books.

Lavelle, Louis (1973), *The Dilemma of Narcissus*, London: George Allen & Unwin Ltd.

Levenkron, Steven (2006), *Cutting: Understanding and Overcoming Self-Mutilation*, New York: W.W. Norton and Company.

Lewis, C.S. ([1960] 1988), *The Four Loves*, New York: Harcourt Brace.

Lewis, C.S. ([1952] 1980), *Mere Christianity*, New York: HarperOne.

MacDonald, Scott (2006), "Petit Larceny, the Beginning of All Sin: Augustine's Theft of the Pears," *Augustine's Confessions: Critical Essays*, ed., William E. Mann, Lanham, MD: Rowman & Littlefield.

Mann, William (2016), *God, Belief, and Perplexity*, Oxford: Oxford University Press.

Manning, Brennan (1982), *A Stranger to Self-Hatred: A Glimpse of Jesus*, Denville, NJ: Dimension Books.

Markus, Robert (1989), *Conversion and Disenchantment in Augustine's Spiritual Cmareer*, Villanova, PA: Villanova University Press.

Martinez, Luis M. ([1949] 2014), *Worshipping a Hidden God: Unlocking the Secrets of the Interior Life*, Manchester, NH: Sophia Institute Press.

Meconi, S.J., David (2013), *The One Christ: St. Augustine's Theology of Deification*, Washington, DC: Catholic University of America Press.

Mele, Alfred R. (2001), *Self-Deception Unmasked*, Princeton: Princeton University Press.

Merton, Thomas (1962), *New Seeds of Contemplation*, New York: New Directions Press.

O'Donnell, James (1992), *Augustine: Confessions*, vol. II: *Commentary on Books 1-7*, Oxford: Clarendon Press.

O'Donovan, Oliver ([1980] 2006), *The Problem of Self-Love in St. Augustine*, Eugene, OR: Wipf and Stock

Otten, Willemien and Susan Schreiner, eds. (2018), *Augustine our Contemporary: Examining the Self in Past and Present*, Notre Dame, IN: Notre Dame University Press.

Paffenroth, Kim and Robert P. Kennedy, eds. (2003), *A Reader's Guide to Augustine's Confessions*, Louisville: Westminster John Knox Press.

Pieper, Josef. ([1962] 1986), *Faith, Hope, Love*, San Francisco: Ignatius Press.

Pope Francis (2013), *Lumen Fidei*, Washington, DC: United States Conference of Catholic Bishops.

Rigby, Paul (2015), *The Theology of Augustine's Confessions*, Cambridge: Cambridge University Press.

Rigby, Paul (2013), "Was Augustine a Narcissist?" *Augustinian Studies* 44:1, 59–91.

Stump, Eleonore (2010), *Wandering in Darkness*, Oxford: Oxford University Press.

Sullivan, O.P. and John Edward (1963), *The Image of God: The Doctrine of St. Augustine and Its Influence*, Dubuque, IA: Priory Press.

Teske, S.J, Roland (2008), "Augustine's Inversion of 1 John 4:8," *Augustinian Studies* 39:1, 49–60.

Weinandy, O.F.M.-Cap., Thomas (2000), *Does God Suffer?* Notre Dame, IN: University of Notre Dame Press.

Wetzel, James. (2013), "Trappings of Woe," *Parting Knowledge: Essays after Augustine*, Eugene, OR: Cascade Books, 58–80.

Wills, Garry (2003), *Saint Augustine's Sin*, New York: Viking Books.

INDEX

Index